Web Designer Side Hustle

Build No-Code websites.
Work from anywhere. And design your life for
freedom.

For step-by-step video training to accelerate income skills go to my course platform at https://member.johnmac.pro/

For resources mentioned in this book, go to:
https://johnmac.pro/book-resources/

Table of Contents

Welcome, genius

Hello, I'm John Mac. Right now I'm having a pretty strong Americano at one of my favorite coffee shops while typing on this book. I actually wrote big parts of it on a couple of plain trips. And while sitting by the pool at a wonderful hotel in Bali. I mention this because it's many people's dream to live a lifestyle like this. But they think it's complicated, too hard, or worse, impossible to see it happen for them.

I'm here to brighten up your mind, inspire, and hopefully teach you something valuable that can bring you greater freedom in life. Similar to what I and many other smart life-hackers have decided to do with their lives:

To not follow the norms. And instead be a creator instead of a follower in the herd of society.

Having you here reading this book means a lot. To me, having people seeking new information to elevate and improve their lives is cool. It's the kind of people I like to have around me. Keeping in mind the words Tony Robbins uses to say:

"You become like the 5 of your closest friends".

It's great to meet people teaching themselves something new, especially so that they become stronger, more aware, and independent in their own reality. And with this growth usually comes the need to find new ways to make money. And to live a life of greater purpose. Which is your birthright. But it's just not taught in school.

And for you to learn a new craft that can become a work-from-home or full-time--while-traveling creative career is one of those brilliant ways to train your mind and educate yourself. This is practical learning where you are in full control. Completely self-paced and outside of our terrible educational system.

Learning to build websites, create designs, write, consult, and other creative online careers is easy to start. And you're gaining new skills and knowledge without society's approval, special tests, or useless grades. You will be grading yourself from now on.

In this short book, I will show you how to start on this path in an easy way. I will share some of my methods and explain how you should take the first steps to build websites you can get paid for. It's a short read to give you an overview of the thinking, tools, and workflows you should use to start creating an income using your laptop.

It will be a simple and excellent read to educate yourself. And what I have learned over time is how few web designers I know around me. So, those times when I'm fully booked with work and I have to turn clients away, they ask me if I know anyone else I could recommend. I usually have to say no.

There's enough work to take on. The choice for you at this point is if you're willing to teach yourself something cool and decide to be the boss and owner of your own success.

Time to choose your own freedom?

I will show you how you can leave your house every morning with your head held high, breathing in the fresh air, and go to your favorite café in town to work on your laptop. A flexible craft that can bring in a nice salary without having a boss.

If you don't drink coffee or crowded cafés, grab a takeaway tea and pretend you're a guest in a hotel lobby. I have done this a few times. Because setting the stage and location for your freedom lifestyle is very important.

My purpose for this book is to give you a good starting point. I want you to see that you alone can set things up to quickly learn how to make an income from building websites without any coding or design skills. That's how I started. And it's even easier today compared to my earlier years.

Besides showing you typical workflows, apps, and tools, I will also teach you how to set up and receive payments to your bank account. We'll be using well-known high-quality services.

The process in this book will get the ball rolling for you to establish a good foundation for how we build websites, the professional way. For me, building websites and getting lots of happy clients became my way to live a dream life.

And it may sound strange to you now, but as soon as you have completed one website job, the next one pops up. That's been my experience over and over again. And it's why I now live on my reputation, and the positive "manifesting flow" of constantly having new jobs coming in.

I have never advertised anything, ever, to try and find more work. I have client abundance. And my wish for you with this beginner's book is to find that flow. It's all about how you present yourself, serve your clients, and because "that Web Designer" customers just like to be in touch with.

And as you keep getting more projects, you'll gain valuable experience, and gradually develop a reputation you can live on.

I will teach you how to start as a Web Designer without any coding skills, design experience, or special technical background. If you follow the steps I'm sharing in this book, you can make a good income the way I do, including passive income.

Earning passive income

If the topic of "recurring" and "passive" income is new to you, here is an example of what I mean by "passive income":

When you work online, there are many ways to create small and large income streams. I have made sure to work smart so that one of my income streams passively pays me about $550 monthly. And it keeps growing, even though I'm not spending much time on it. The greatest benefit of passive income is to have money flowing in even when you are asleep.

By counting the number of hours I put in to receive that specific payment, I would say it's worth it. And I'd say it's truly passive income.

Why? Because I work 0 hours for it!

That's a fact. And I will tell you how I did it.

A few years back, while being early into playing with WordPress as a tool to build websites, I discovered Shopify–the top, world-renowned e-commerce platform.

One of the clients I had at the time wanted to sell online. So they asked me to build an e-commerce website. I did some research and discovered Shopify. And after setting up a couple of Shopify stores for clients, the Shopify partner team reached out and suggested I become a "Shopify Expert." So I joined and became both a "Partner" and Shopify Expert.

The first and only one in Norway at that time.

When building e-commerce websites as a Shopify Partner and Expert, we get a certain percentage from the client stores we set up. We get paid twice a month. And for me, building many stores and working with a long list of clients adds up over time. My current partner income is about $550 monthly for Shopify stores that are still active and selling. And that is just ONE passive income stream.

How would another income stream change your quality of life and your freedom?

It's a nice bonus to have while doing other well-paid one-time website projects. And this was just one example of "passive income". There are many ways to build income streams like this. And it's especially convenient as a web designer. Because in this industry, recurring and passive income streams are common.

So learning how to build websites and cultivate happy clients opens you up to more financial freedom. Here's what a new stream of self-made income could do:

- ✓ You could buy a brand-new Mac laptop for your work (recommended).
- ✓ Travel somewhere exotic, or maybe to Iceland (recommended). Let journeys like this inspire you and your work.
- ✓ Afford to work, eat, and enjoy more time out.
- ✓ Buy something nice for a friend or partner.
- ✓ Buy access to online courses and training to become even better at your craft and skills (which will improve your business).
- ✓ Order a Bose noise-canceling headset to have peace while working in cafés and in public spaces. (Like airplanes.)
- ✓ Buy new clothes and shoes to match your entrepreneurial lifestyle as a freelance online business owner. It will strengthen your personal brand.

If you can picture living this lifestyle and having this freedom, this book can easily become your first map and support for this journey.

I will be repeating the topic of mindset. Because it's a big deal if you really WANT to achieve goals and meaningful dreams in life. It's what you should aim for. Another business I run is specialized 1-1 coaching and mindset re-programming. So it's part of me, and it's a passion cultivated further from my 17 years of martial arts.

So let me continue with a few important notes regarding mindset and belief systems. These are topics I cover a lot in my mindset coaching. Because it has a huge impact on the results people will have in their lives.

Have the mindset not to follow the sheep

To set a new direction towards a life of freedom and smarter income, the question will be, do you have the mindset?

Your mindset is all about the program that's currently activated in your mind. It runs your life. It's a blueprint program that dictates your beliefs, which dictate your choices you make in your life. And it's all stuffed into your head by your parents, the school system, media, and politics. Plus other mind-twisting institutions that have been allowed to influence humanity's minds on this planet for a long time.

I'm hoping that you will set the intention and decide that making a positive change in your life CAN and WILL create new results.

I'm talking about your inner voice and what thoughts will be mumbling in the back of your head. In relation to learning the skills presented in this book, my videos, and my courses, it should be feelings of excitement and clear intentions.

One of the reasons I love helping people make a living from their personal qualities and skills is to show them that following the "system" is not a ticket to happiness.

And let's be honest, the "normal" in society is not exactly giving us butterflies in our stomach. Most people's goals and intentions are weak, and usually adopted from previous generations. Or copied from the template funnel where we stand nicely in line waiting for school to begin. Then perform and present to the best of your ability with no individualism or evaluation.

I guess I'm pretty much a "rebel of the norms." It's what has brought me much greater freedom. It has been a lonely journey at times. But I will rather elevate, grow, and build my freedom in my cave. And then mingle with like-minded people who think for themselves when I feel like it.

I'm certainly not the typical guy in the street. I don't live the conventional life, have a regular job, or follow the conventional "script" most people blindly obey and comply with. I operate on a different level. So, my reality is different. You will discover great things if you have the courage to walk away from a flock of sheep. Following the herd is not the right way if you want to do great things. Going your way, figuring out the path, and declaring yourself the most important person in your life will shift you into that reality you dream of.

I prefer meeting other people who live with an elevated worldview and have higher expectations for life. The mindset they have is different. And sometimes, I help them grow, feel more confident, and find better ways to make a living. By doing that, they can have their freedom, independence, and build the future they want.

To me, the educational system sucked. Working to survive in a nine-to-five, flat-salary job is not for me. That's why I quit my job many years ago and have been working on my freedom business ever since. It's simple. You only need a computer and Internet connection for many of the crafts and types of work you can do online.

I have met so many people with valuable, high-quality skills they don't use. Instead, they dance to the squeaky pipe of "normalism" and hope it will make them happy. Again, they do what most of their friends, family, and the society around them do–the daily grind in the conventional system. Playing the same song day after day.

Free yourself and create something new

If you can relate to being one of the free souls looking for higher meaning, freedom, purpose, and better ways of making a living, being a follower won't work. You have to step out and lead your way. Go with those who think similar thoughts, and you will fly.

Having this mindset early on is why I eventually dropped out of that burning carousel of the "normal life". I wanted to own my ship and sail wherever I wanted. The first opportunity for birthing this lifestyle started to develop when I grew as a Web Designer.

And since 2018, I also focused more on my other business. Mindset coaching elevating people's mindset, personal growth, and spiritual awakening. It has a huge impact on body and mind. People start doing magic when expanding their understanding on this level.

So, it helps to have the right mindset. Not because this book is complex or Web Design is complicated. But if you're like most people, you may fall victim to the instant gratification of the mind. And give up before the good life starts.

Everybody has a greater potential than they think. We all have various reasons to be the way we are. Especially with the current state of the planet and how most of us are presented with false truths and bad education from childhood. It leaves us with a fearful and weak mind and a shallow foundation for life.

As you may know, some people quit before they even start. The reason could be that their dream was not strong enough, or they think less of themselves and their ability to make things happen in life. This is fine and quite common.

To decide that you can't do great things in life is also a choice. But you still have the option to think differently. Don't be like most other people, be extraordinary. Don't be a follower. Be a leader. At least of your very own life story.

Stand out. Not for other people, but for yourself. Be different. Don't copy. Be unique.

It can be scary to stand out. But when you do, life will bring about a lot more magic. It also feels a lot better, and it's a hell of a lot healthier than simply bowing, obeying, and saying "yes, master" to your family, friends, government, or any other system you give your life-force away to.You may have heard Steve Jobs (Apple) famously say:

> "Here's to the crazy ones, the misfits, the rebels, the troublemakers, the round pegs in the square holes... the ones who see things differently -- they're not fond of rules...
>
> You can quote them, disagree with them, glorify or vilify them, but the only thing you can't do is ignore them because they change things...
>
> They push the human race forward, and while some may see them as the crazy ones, we see genius because the ones who are crazy enough to think that they can change the world are the ones who do."
>
> -Steve Jobs.

Okay, thats it for this introduction and topic of mindset. Maybe its not that important to you. But having a growth-mindset will for sure accelerate your learning, wins, and results of your dreams.

Here's what you get

Take a quick look at what you can expect from this book and how our journey will unfold.

How we think becomes our reality. And my way of teaching people will always include a certain level of ideas, tips, and knowledge of mindset rewriting. Scientists also know that learning new things will develop and expand the neurons in our brains. And that will also be the result of this book.

Now, besides mind and brain goodies. Here are the main takeaways and my goals for you with this book and training.

✓ To say YES to your dreams of having a new freelance or work-from-anywhere lifestyle. And bring in at least one new income stream.

✓ To build a new website for yourself and use it as a reference.

✓ Get your first paid client project sooner rather than later.

Does that sound doable and possible for you? Keep in mind, if you don't manage to get your first paid website project rather soon, don't get discouraged. It's part of the process. And at the same time, it's up to you how fast you want to move forward.

What is important here is that you will learn how to register domains and set up websites. Then you suddenly have a lucrative skill. And that's when opportunities happen. They will come. Now, here's what else you can expect from this book.

Getting clarity on becoming a web designer

Having clarity and awareness is good. It makes you more confident. In our context, I will help you understand the concept of you being a Web Designer and what that means. Why and how you can relate to the craft of being a designer, page-builder, or...

A Web Designer. Part of your skills will be to have this industry awareness. I think this chapter will make you feel good about this craft and put you on the map.

A quick setup of up your first website

We will start pretty quickly with going through where and how to register your first domain and install WordPress on it. WordPress is the free open-source CMS platform you will have access to for free. And use to build all your client websites.

Find clients and getting paid

Are you confident enough to ask for payments from your future clients?

This is a serious question and a hot topic. We're touching on some delicate mindset concepts again that affect many new freelancers: **To get properly paid.** So, we'll have two chapters preparing our minds to accept "abundance" and being paid. And also how we start looking for clients and projects to work on. And for that, we also need to talk about pricing. An area that is not too easy to teach from a book I would say, but I will at least provide some good tips to get you started in the right way.

Setting up workflows and gathering the tools

Enjoying your work while building websites is going to be important. And to set yourself up with a fun and productive environment has a big impact on your joy factor. We don't really need much to build websites. But with the tools we use, we should make sense of them and enjoy using them. If a long-haul truck driver doesn't love his truck and its interior, he will dislike his job and suffer from spending night and day at his job along the road.

It's the same for us. Our devices and tools should be a joy and fun experience to work with. I will help suggest what you can use. And I will share what I use in my business. But over time, you will have to try out different tools yourself so you can settle with what you like to use.

Links to resources and tools

There are thousands of tools, apps, services, techniques, and technologies in the landscape of web design and online business. So it's going to be important that you start off with the right setup. To save you from 96% of unnecessary technology jungle madness, I will guide you on what tools and services to use.

It's going to save you a lot of trial and testing, time, and even money.

There will be some links to be found throughout this book. Some of these links will be my affiliate links, which may include discounts and benefits. Make sure to use them so you don't miss out. Plus, you're helping me as a hustling author.

One important note for you here: affiliate links are also an example of how you should think about your online work in the future. You will start growing your passive income by sharing affiliate links with your clients and followers.

I wrote a short book about it also. It's to introduce you to recurring and passive income. And help build more steady revenue streams. It has all the tips and methods I use to earn affiliate income from clients I already serve. And it's a great start if you are new to the words "affiliate" and "passive income." It's important information for any one-person business. And something you will be happy you got to learn about.

Unless you already got this book as part of a bundle, go get the: "**A Web Designer's Playbook to Build Recurring Passive Income**" from the resources page on my site.

Besides apps and suggestions for online services, I want you to pay extra attention to what I suggest in regards to WordPress plugins and themes. Those two things are what will be your primary building blocks to set up high-quality websites. And there are thousands of these, and it's very easy to pick bad themes and plugins.

Professional WordPress web designers usually have a good knowledge and predefined list of plugins they want to use for various projects. And I will provide you with what I use, so you can start with a good selection for your first projects. I will explain more important details later in the book about what WordPress themes and plugins really are.

Tips to keep the cost low

You can also expect to begin this journey with minimal investment with this book. You can start building websites and get paid at nearly no cost at all. But I will not teach you how to create high-quality and professional work by showing you the cheapest ways of building things online. Let's at least have some minimal standards for ourselves. And for our reputation.

Usually, to start a "business" in the way we typically perceive it equals a vast money-hoarding practice and investment. Hell, some people take up loans, sell their souls, their bodies, or their stuff to go all-in on some risky business adventure. At the same time, they are dependent on investors that have to believe in their idea.

But in the case of you starting out learning web design from a coffee shop, none of that is needed. Your first "investment" may have been this very book. And the cost has been ridiculously low.

Next, you only need a computer and an Internet connection. Something you most likely already have. If not, let's say you at least have a laptop. Then go to a hotel lobby, library, or café to educate yourself.

With this book, you're not dependent on anybody's money investment. You're the owner of your own damn ship at this point. Because the cash needed to start THIS kind of online business is within reach for everyone. Let's do a quick checkup of what necessary tools you will need.

1. **Do you have a computer? (A device)**
2. **Got access to the Internet? (A location)**
3. **Do you have the freedom to make clever choices for yourself? (A brain)**

If you can check off these three items, you are ready to go. Glory be to your awesomeness. Now let's all hold hands and sing Kumbaya. Because it all starts now.

Here's an entrepreneur life hack:

Free Internet Wi-Fi spots can be found anywhere. If you don't have Wi-Fi at home, dress a little sexy, and bring a cup of takeaway tea to enjoy in a hotel lobby somewhere. You're on a business trip! If the receptionist asks if they can help you, kindly reply that you're doing awesome and are just waiting on a business meeting. And then you end with this:

"By the way, I bet you know someone that would need a new website, yes?"...

I have done this many times. It puts me in a good mind-state being at a hotel instead of a local café. Back in the days, the local coffee shop was a place where too many people... knew me. And they all wanted to talk. But I didn't. So I walked 200m to the Nearby, I sat down in the lobby. Suddenly, I was on a journey building my future!

You could also go to the library for free Wi-Fi and work there. Or, modern gas stations even often have Wi-Fi now. Just make sure you use a VPN when you're out and about.

After being in this industry for many years, I know the typical expenses and costs of working as a freelancer. I like to have the right tools, apps, and services to make my business flow more productively and fun. Quality apps are important to me.

But with the tips and training in this book, I aim to keep the cost low for you. The "investment" we're talking about here is the bare minimum and so affordable that you could pick up and turn in empty soda bottles to make it happen.

I will give you links to the tools, services, and platforms you need to get started. Some are free, and some are paid.

But, I won't be recommending only free tools just because they are free. Sometimes it's a good idea to actually pay for a quality hammer instead of getting a free one that bends after two hits. Setting yourself up with certain standards in your craft makes you feel better about your workday and towards your clients.

Invest in your devices and tools. It makes you stand out with a quality signature. It's like comparing a carpenter rigged with professional tools versus one who bought it all at a toy store. Which one are you?

Starting a project and further advice

In the last part of this book, I will teach some fundamental workflows to start off your first client project. Staying organized with this will help you stay in control and make work more fun.

Then I will share some words of encouragement to build confidence and a stronger belief in your goals. And suggest some ideas to learn faster and get paid better.

When you are ready to accelerate the learning and shorten the time between building your first website and getting paid, visit https://member.johnmac.pro/.

Now, pick a café and let's dive in.

Getting you started as a web designer

Before you start river-dancing in excitement, let's get some clarity of who you will become on this journey.

You may go right ahead and overdo yourself at your own will and plow through this book in one day. But I suggest trying out things at a healthy pace. Read, feel, and mentally picture yourself growing new skills at this point. Not only technical skills, but also a new level of awareness. You are self-educating now. So you can freely move on at your own pace.

Many people are seeking new ways to make a solid income. This can be done in different ways. You could try to switch jobs. But often you would just find yourself doing something else you don't really care about. And being stuck, yet again, with a flat salary that never goes up.

So then, one alternative way to make a living is to NOT serve another master, but creating value and offering your own skills directly to customers. That's when you avoid being the employee who just gets a "salary" while the company takes the rest. Sailing your own ship means you get paid directly for your services with a much higher hourly rate or project price.

Maybe you have a job or you go to school, but dream about starting a side gig. And it could be that you're just damn tired of whatever you're into and want to quit. Which is a very common thing. Then, Web Design is one of the easiest ways to make a shift from employee to a one-man business. I'm not just glorifying my own craft and industry here.

Web Design, and similar skills and crafts for digital content, has a pretty easy point of entry. And here's why:

✓ There are no degrees or official education needed.

✓ Learning the skills you want is abundantly available online.

✓ The cost to start learning and building is extremely low.

So if it's this easy to get started, what could be the challenge here?

You. It's all about how much you want it. If something is important to us in life, humans find enormous power and strength to get what they desire. Keep your dreams fueled with a fire of desire. And remember that crowds of people have walked the same path before you and enjoyed the process. And so can you.

So, let's move on and go through a few topics adding some more knowledge to your mind as you become a Web Designer.

Shifting from a flat salary to a lucrative one-man freedom business

I know a few people who are happy with their current job. And that is wonderful. You may be at the right place and love what you do. And then it's all good. If you're happy with the work you do, you're in a good flow and you should stay with that.

But the challenge is that it seems like most people are NOT happy with their jobs. A lot of surveys have been conducted on this topic. And if you are like **the**

70-80% of the population who can't stand their daily job, I still wouldn't just recommend to "ditch" what you do now and lose your current income.

That would just be like brutally firing yourself in an uncontrolled emotional reaction while kicking the trash bin on the way out.

Instead, be clever. Stick with it for some time while staying motivated and secretly working on your new side hustle and your ticket to freedom. And so it will be that the day of liberation will come. Your last grumpy morning as a peasant will arrive. And the final words uttered from your firm lips will be: "I'm done". You will drop the mic and leave the stage. And while exiting the institution that shall never be spoken of again, you confidently tell your boss to stuff your salary where the sun never shines.

And from now on the warmth of the morning sunrise will shine in your face again, and a new journey has begun.

Okay, maybe I got carried away for a moment there, while reflecting on the last employee job that I had. I was in flight-mode the day I quit my job! I believe I was even a few grams lighter, physically.

Now, not everybody is in a bad place with their current job. And the goal of starting a side hustle would be more to add a second stream of income. Which also is a great idea. Maybe you got a part-time job and want to fill the remaining hours with a meaningful project that will bring greater financial freedom. At least towards a profitable hobby that can bring in some extra cash for whatever dreams you have.

You never know. It could bring enough cache for you to buy a new microphone so you can start singing your own song instead of squeaking to somebody else's tune.

Setting up your first website

Are you ready to set up your website and have an online platform that will profile you as a Web Designer and generate an income? What's your business name going to be? How about your logo? How do you move on if a potential client contacts you from your website?

Well, let's try to keep our pants on and walk mindfully towards the end goal for this book. You will get answers to the questions above later in the book. And you may find it a lot easier to set things up than what you have pictured already.

Let me just say that getting your own website set up is not urgent at all. You don't really need to have a website ready to take on your first client projects. You won't need a degree in anything. And previous client testimonials are not necessary. I have done a lot of client work without having to show off anything. The trust in my words while introducing myself and sharing my advice and knowledge was all it took.

For now, the reason and what we should focus on in regards to setting up your own website is for practice and experience. And over time, you can decide if you want to keep your website or not.

My explanations in this book will be simple, and I will keep things short. There won't be many choices regarding what tools, services, and workflow methods to use because I aim to have you copy what's been working well for me. When you do, I know you can create something that will bring the same income as I have built for myself. There is no point in complicating things.

That would just frustrate you and end up in a burn-out over time.

If you're a beginner trying to figure things out by yourself, it will end up in confusion and chaos. There is a 90% chance you would make so many wrong turns that you could end up at the house of horror, tossing your laptop away and running screaming into the forest at night.

The next morning you'll wake up on some green moss, cold and afraid. And the dream of passive income, freedom, and building cool stuff on coffeeshops was just a bad dream.

If I just prompted you to do the following:

- Find a good hosting company - where would you go?
- Install WordPress - How would you start?
- Pick a WordPress theme - you would have to choose between thousands of them. And they would all be shitty cheap themes not worth your time.
- You need a form builder plugin for this project - how would you be able to select a good plugin that's well made and easy to use?
- WordPress themes are crap, you need a page-builder - What is that and which one should you use?

This book won't give you the ultimate list of tools you could use. But instead, it will get you started fast using the proper tools and workflows that I know are safe. By having me tell you what steps to take, which services to go for, and what tools to pick, you'll fly faster than if you would fiddle around alone in the dark.

So the remedy for the bad dream is this book. It contains enough guidance and pointers for beginners to safely transform themselves into a skilled digital craftsman that can build sexy websites that could pay out everything from $1000 to $10,000. (or more). And after (or while) you have read this book, it's time for some simple tutorial videos to see how quickly a site can be built.

Make sure to pay a visit to my course platform to get training and lessons perfectly matching this book. And to follow the path suggested to make a new income that can grow over time.

Since you will be starting as a WordPress Web Designer with a proper setup, you will master this craft much quicker. And enjoy the process sooner. I would be pleased to see you get to that point quickly.

So here's what to plan for and accomplish in the next chapters.

- Pick a reasonably priced and quality hosting service for your website.
- Set up your WordPress website and install a design theme (free).
- Add pages and content to the website.
- Set up a system to have clients pay you (free).

To achieve these goals, I'll recommend tools and services that I confidently believe would suit you as a new Web Designer. These are tools and services I use in my work and those my team has been trained to use.

Of course, I'll differentiate between lower-cost and simpler tools to more advanced and slightly more expensive ones. It depends on your current work. For instance, choosing an advanced VPS hosting service to manage the server is unnecessary and overwhelming. It's a bad plan and a wrong choice of service.

Instead, let's go for the right tools and services at this point.

Prepare to have a paid client job.

You should start connecting with people and local businesses immediately. Start now, and put the word and energy out there about your new "personal project" that you have going on. Let's aim to have ONE project for anybody needing a website.

This may sound scary at first. Will you be able to handle such a job? Well, my advice here is that you will select a project that sounds simple and easy to do:

A simple website that has no fancy or advanced technical integrations. But simply images and text. And maybe set up for a blog. The blog functionality is already built into WordPress. So you would basically only add content.

Just planting the seed in people (potential customers) that you meet can bounce back with an opportunity for a simple project without you having to "sell" anything. It could even be for a friend that has a hobby or just wants a simple blog.

We will talk about payment and how to handle that later.

Now, let's continue with more tips that will be good to know when starting as a new Web Designer. I want you to get the picture right. So you can begin with a good foundational overview of the craft. Of course, there are many paths, methods, and areas within web design. But again, we will focus on WordPress page-building and the workflows I make a living off. So you can copy that.

Let's define the title "Web Designer".

If you call yourself a Web designer, what are you really then? A programmer? Are you a designer? Do you draw and sketch on a Moleskine notebook with a pencil, looking smart and creative?

The label has become an eye-catching title for a craft with many different areas. And you will most likely NOT become a "web designer."

Or maybe you do! For the love of creation, what do I know?

In that case, are you prepared to be a graphical UI/UX designer for the web? Working with apps like Figma, Photoshop, Sketch, and even pen and paper?

Technically, that is what a "web designer" is. It's a craft where you are not building websites but designing for those who DO build websites. This book is intended to help you learn how to work with the technical side of things. Not just design the mock-up and graphics, and deliver a final graphics. Because technically, that is what a Web Designer is.

I wanted to bring this up because it's important for you to know the difference and ensure you put yourself in the right box. Knowing the difference will already get you educated on the terms around this craft of building websites.

Now, at the same time, you CAN call yourself a Web Designer. Because you WILL be using a WordPress page-builder and whatever build-in "design" options you have in any of those builders. But to be correct, a designer designs stuff. It's a different craft. And with that, I will also mention that any person who calls themselves a Web Designer should know HOW to build websites and understand the concepts and the building blocks for typical website solutions. A designer who knows the building blocks HTML structure of a website will craft the design for it in the right way.

So, in regards to the purpose of this book and what you will learn, you're not going to be a designer. Unless that is what you will also put your focus on. Which is great. And beneficial.

The next thing that you are NOT is a **Web Developer**. If you are a "developer," you're a coder who develops and codes solutions for the web, doing programming. This is most likely not what you will be getting into.

Unless you do. Lightning may strike, and maybe you find it exciting. And in that case, you will be a Web Designer who knows development and coding. Which will bring enormous skill levels and strength.

But, becoming a designer nor coder is necessary for the methods you'll be learning through this book. And still, you can become a highly skilled craftsman building advanced websites with a high price tag.

So, I think we can say that if you are neither a web "Designer" nor Web Developer, what are you?

"WHO AM I?"....

No need to scream in desperation. Let's sit down, meditate for a moment, and get to know ourselves.

I guess you can call yourself a "website builder." That should cover it. We're not stepping on the designer's or developers' sensitive toes.

Not that we care. So I can say, for my part, I call myself a Web Designer. It's simple, and people know what it is. And to be correct, I also sketch and use Figma for some of my design work before I build it on WordPress. I also do lots of custom CSS coding because I like it. CSS code handles how things LOOK on your websites, and it's easy to learn. You might like it.

But even if I don't do manual sketched and graphical design work before I build a website, my title is a Web Designer. And you should continue to use the title "Web Designer" from now on. Because that is the overall title used for people that design or build websites. It's also a title that is the easiest for you to start earning a living from since it is a common title that clients and companies recognize. There is no reason to elaborate or explain otherwise unless it becomes a question. In that case, you would already know your technical skills and workflows to explain accordingly.

Or, tell your clients: I'm a Web Crafter (™ my idea)

What skills do you need to build websites?

I want to be clear with you and help you get a better picture of what you need to know to build websites in these "modern times." It's simpler than you think. But you can go more advanced when you feel ready and want to.

What I mean is, it has just become way much easier than before. We use more platforms, tools, and plugins to build sites. That makes it easier. But more advanced technology also exists, so you can also build websites in a more custom and advanced way. The advanced and custom way is not our path. We will be using platforms, tools, and plugins.

You'll love it.

So I will quickly go through a list of basic skills, tools, and services you will be using–the typical "tech stack" and the workflows around it. And what I'm teaching you here will be with a professional approach in mind.

I won't show you services like Wix, Webflow, Squarespace, or other platforms you must rent and pay for. They are limited, and your clients won't own their website platform. And using services like that tends to produce terrible HTML code in the background. There's also often a bunch of tracking code running in the background that you haven't asked for. Nope, we will build to own our platform.

Here's a short list of tools and services you will gain skills around.

- Platform: WordPress - Its free and open source
- WordPress design themes - Free and some paid
- WordPress page-builders - 100% customizable themes

To continue building your dream and create new income by building websites, here's a list of qualities you need to have.

- Know how to use your computer and access the Internet.
- Have the capacity to learn something new.
- Being able to find help on YouTube by doing a search.
- Know what a web browser is (like Chrome or Safari) and understand that there are many of them. (Brave, Firefox, Edge, Opera, Min)

I'm pretty sure these are personal skills you already have. So as you see, it doesn't take too much to be able to build websites.

Next, don't freak out just because you don't recognize the words or titles just yet. Here are five new things you're about to level up on to build websites.

1. What domains and hosting are all about (Not hard).
2. What WordPress is and how to use it (Easy).
3. How WordPress themes and page builders work (Easy).
4. Plugins and extensions for WordPress (Easy).
5. Some apps to manage your jobs and get paid (Not hard).

You will quickly learn more about these as we go on through the book here. Also, a quick YouTube search will bring some clear answers. Or, you could ask ChatGPT like this:

"Please give a simple answer and explanation on what domains are and how they work. Please explain like I'm 7 years old."

Next, I will quickly run through and expand on some of the steps we will be going through in the process of this book. This is beginner-level information. If the following sub-topics are familiar to you, just skip this.

Selecting a good hosting company

A hosting company is where you store and run your website. Some of them also offer domain registration, and some do not. And there are online services that only focus on domain registration. Sometimes it's reasonable and necessary to register the domain in one place and host the website elsewhere. I will give you a few options later. And show you what could be a good option for your clients.

Since 2021, I started offering my own premium WordPress hosting for my clients. We call it WPAlchemy, and it's a perfect place to host your WordPress website in a more "premium" way. We won't be using our service for the training in this book. But feel free to have a look at what we do here.

Visit WPAlchemy.io

What WordPress is and how to use it

WordPress is a free "app" that runs on a hosting server. Initially, it started as a pretty simple and flexible application to start a blog. It quickly became popular and has expanded enormously. It's now powering a massive part of all the Internet's websites. In fact, as much as over 65% of the whole Internet. You can even download WordPress for free and run it on your computer. Something I teach you how to do in my course platform. The course is called "Master LocalWP: Fast-Track Your WordPress Site Development".

Important Note: Never go to **wordpress.com** and start a website project. That is a totally different, paid service. Instead, we use WordPress.org. And, usually, we don't even go to that website. WordPress is already provided by the hosting companies I will be suggesting for you in this book. It's just a few clicks to install, and you are ready to go. So hold on until we go through that setup and installation.

This is also important knowledge to know about when speaking to your future clients. It's not an uncommon thing that some clients will think that they should "obviously" go to WordPress.com.

How WordPress themes and page builders work

A new WordPress installation looks boring and useless. Though technically, it's perfectly usable with its default install and the free WordPress theme. But it looks just incredibly sad, boring, and not much inviting.

So to create a better design, we can pick a "theme" to change the look and feel of the site. This feature is already built into WordPress when you log in. It's quick and simple to do, and will get you going setting up a website super-fast. When choosing design themes, you can pick from thousands of both free and paid WordPress themes.

But using themes is not the recommended workflow if you really want to have control of the design of the website you are building. So, instead, we use a different type of WordPress theme (or plugin).

We call them "page-builders," and they are much more powerful. By using a page builder, you can design and customize websites exactly how your clients want them. This would not be possible using a standard theme. Because they are predefined, I guess we could say.

When building websites using a proper page-builder, you can charge a much higher price for your work. It's a lot more fun to work with. And you can "design" with way more options than a fixed and limited free theme. I never use WordPress themes anymore. It's too limited. Even for simple jobs.

So for all my client projects, I use page-builders like Bricks Builder. Also Oxygen Builder is an awesome choice as it is producing proper HTML markup and code. There are other known page-builders for WordPress. But it's not something I will recommend. Remember: You have to consider yourself a professional from the start. Not a consumer trying to hack something up on their own with click-and-drag.

Plugins and extensions for WordPress

Usually, when building websites, you typically want specific functions, features, and more useful functionalities. Like contact forms, image galleries, or even membership features. You can even install a full e-commerce setup in WordPress for FREE. Expanding functions and cool features in WordPress is easy to do. Just pick a "plugin," install it right inside WordPress, and you are good to go. There are thousands of free plugins and endless premium and paid plugins. Which, which, again, is often a better choice. Choosing what plugins to use can be confusing. So I will be recommending good plugins for you to choose from.

Themes and plugins for WordPress live in a crazy jungle. So it's better to get started with some well-known quality plugins instead of trying things out among thousands of shitty plugins.

An app to manage your jobs and get paid

Let me just take a sip of my coffee here and share something with you.

I'm an app geek.

I love having good workflows and a nice overview of my projects and tasks. I love productivity and a clean workspace. A clean and functional app to organize your website projects and tasks will help you gain more control of your work and step-by-step process. I will suggest good apps and services to use. Not just to plan and organize your work. But to start off with a certain level of control and professionalism. That raises confidence and your capacity to manage your projects and tasks in an orderly manner. I will also go over how you can set yourself up to get paid from your clients. So that you have a solid and smooth money flow.

What you don't need to build websites

One of the reasons it's been a joy to write this book is to help you see that building professional websites is no longer about writing code and manually typing HTML, CSS, or any other programmatic poetry. You certainly can if you so desire. But like I already mentioned, then you are moving into website development.

I would like to reinforce your understanding and confidence in two topics which often are common questions for beginners. Coding and design skills. And I will explain why we don't need those skills to build well-paid websites.

When I started writing the first version of this book, I invited a few beta-readers to have them get a taste of it before it was finished. I didn't expect nearly 60 people to sign up in three days. And the questions they provided when joining the beta-readers group were interesting.

One comment or question that kept coming back again and again was:

"I fear the struggle of having to learn coding and HTML..."

I have the power and magic to take away that fear and pain right now. And if you look at the cover of this book, it clearly says you won't need any coding or design skills. And that is the way it is.

The world has changed. The days of fumbling with HTML, PHP, JavaScript, and other code poetry are over. We still do it. And developers are still needed. But in this case, that would only be for special-need and custom client projects.

As I said, this doesn't mean that programming and coding are dead. But let developers be developers and have them hack their poetry in code while you build your websites visually. If you need some special features at any point in the future, you'll be using a plugin to build that functionality. Or you connect with a developer to help you with that task.

But, for the most part, whatever functions you need for your website, there will usually already be a plugin. And this is what coders do. They create modules and functions and extend WordPress's functionality by creating plugins for us.

The next topic was also a common question from my beta readers. And it's something that still tends to come up now and then:

Can I become a Web designer without any design education or experience?

Yes, you certainly can. And many people are already doing it. Just like coders, designers also have a particular interest. They see, feel, and know design-specific details, composition, layouts, and colors that influence the look and feel of a piece of work.

Of course, if you like, design fundamentals are even easier to learn than programming. And resources to learn the basics can be found online. But it is not something you need to spend time on now. We will be using themes and page builders. And with that, the design has already been done.

Later I recommend taking a look at nice websites you like. And try to recreate them in a page builder of your choice by using sections, rows, and modules. Sometimes when I work for myself or my clients, I like to sketch a layout with my notebook and pen. I picture how the design should be based on what the client needs.

But the most common workflow for me is to ask the clients for 2-3 links to websites they like. Then I know what to base work on. Simple and effective.

One of the fun features of Bricks Builder and Oxygen Builder is their built-in library of existing designs. In a page builder, we call them templates. And there's a massive list of free templates to click, install, and modify. You can easily set up a page in a few minutes.

These templates are professionally and beautifully designed. And ready for you to use on any client website you are building. So, you don't need any design skills, but you DO need to know how to use your computer mouse to point and click.

I hope this makes sense. It's important to cover these topics in a solid way so you can see that building a WordPress website at this point in time is more about understanding what LEGO blocks to put together. And this is what this book is based on. Understanding the tools and how to put them together.

Getting help and support to grow your income

The school system fails to teach about discovering your best abilities, managing money, or developing a mindset for success.

A nd this is the most common scenario for most of us that went to a conventional schooling system. You're left to yourself and your capacity to figure out life, reality truths, and your capabilities to do great things in life.

Me spending 17 years of martial arts (Taekwon-Do) training made a big difference in my life. I have truly enjoyed that arena for personal education much more than school. Taekwon-Do training, becoming a leader, and passing several degrees above 1. Dan black belt put me on a figure-shit-out mentality. While at the same time building my own income online. It trained me to cultivate and manage a lot of different skills related to productivity, working with clients, and discovering what's possible when you finally decide to sail your own ship.

The figure-shit-out mentality

I had to figure things out on my own after a nasty childhood, up to 17 years old. Moving away and getting rid of my fifth stepfather was a blessing. Later, from age 18, I lived alone with my dog in an old countryside house that was falling apart. If it rained heavily outside, it was also raining inside. But I felt safer having my dog around. Being the two of us was nice. But it didn't take long until we were three family members.

You see, one day my dear neighbor decided, so lovingly, to share his last chicken with me. Yes, ma'am! One Saturday, after the truck that collects all the birds in his farmhouse had left, ONE clever Jason Bourne chicken had managed to hide. And avoid joining the other feathers on their journey to winged-heaven where the evergreen pastures of golden seeds await.

So, what could he do with this clever ninja chicken? Well, that Saturday evening, I walked home with a chicken under my arm. We became friends. It laid eggs. And we all had a good time.

True story. But I drifted off. Now let's continue.

The point of that story was meant as an example of that: no matter the background, there are ways to make life fantastic without following the "system". The solution is to think for yourself and cultivate the figure-shit-out mentality.

I never took on any formal education, as they call it. Instead, I spent two years at a private school learning Multimedia Design. But even that place had a terrible reputation. Over time, I became more of a helper teacher than a student. Later, the faculty shut down in my city. At that point, I had my own office and spent time helping the few students that were left before they closed the doors. I made sure to steal a couple of books on the craft I was supposed to learn as a compensation for being another sad place to get an education.

As long as you decide that you're smarter than what school says you are, you'll be fine. Educate yourself, cultivate the figure-shit-out mentality, and rock on. And to find help along the way, there are endless sources for help in the age we're currently living in.

Don't ignore customer support

You will learn to use a few tools, apps, and online services. For example, the hosting company and other services you sign up for, their customer support will gladly help you out when you're stuck.

You could ask them, "How do I activate SSL on my domain?" They will either guide you or do it for you. It's always in customer support's best interest to make sure you enjoy their service and will stay as a customer.

The great YouTube oracle.

Did you know that YouTube is the number two search engine in the world? Of course. Because it's owned by Google.

I believe YouTube also has become one of the biggest education platforms in the world. You can learn almost anything on video.

Using the right search words on YouTube will most likely give you what you are looking for. And if you're stuck on any of the topics in this book, I'm sure you will find the answers on YouTube. Though, I think it shouldn't be needed.

Remember, if you find some of the things you now learn a bit challenging, don't think it's unique to you. Someone else has already faced the same bump in the road and will most likely have the answer for you. The methods and techniques we work with are also used by other professionals. So it's easy to find videos and IA chat answers to all of it.

The various help docs.

I know reading documentation is more boring than waiting for a fake plastic plant to bloom. So, that's why we skip that and go do YouTube. Watching videos is fun, and way more effective (usually) than searching and reading for hours.

But remember that there are good tips and insights in the documentation and help sections for the services and tools you use. It would give you the most correct and up-to-date answers to your questions. And it can be precisely what you need when you find yourself stuck. By spending a few minutes on it, you

WILL learn something valuable. And coming directly from the source of the service you are using, you can expect to get the most precise information.

Ask and learn from a Facebook group.

There are a ton of Facebook groups that help people grow a work-from-home business online. Also, for new Web designers and WordPress users. It's all free, and you should be able to find some good answers. Also, make sure to share some of your knowledge and offer help to other members of these groups. When you share your knowledge, other people will support you as well. And if you can be a teacher for a moment, you raise your own skills and confidence.

And as spoiled as you are, here are a few general groups on Facebook for Web designers. Let's hope they are still operative after I finish this book. Thought, to be honest...

I don't like Facebook and haven't used it for years. I find support and advice from AI, Discord groups, Circle communities and such. But, if you're on Facebook and don't mind the platform, you will for sure find some good groups with the topic of Web Design, freelancing and work-from-home learning.

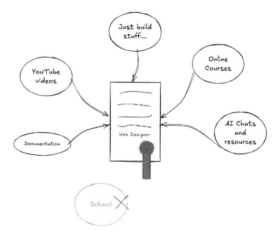

Not to forget - AI tools

As you most likely know, AI has been getting an insane amount of focus the last few years. Various AI models and packages are baked into every other tool and app you can find. What will this lead to? We don't know. But maybe we should at least consider what Elon Musk has been saying for a few years. (Search on YouTube)

When it comes to design and coding, AI has really taken over a lot in those areas as well. But not fully replaced. AI is not emotional (yet). And I would say, a designer emotionally understands design concepts that AI won't.

For coding, AI has become an incredible big part of software development and the daily life workflows for coders and developers. I use it myself. But for you, I think AI will be the most important tool to get quick and specific answers to questions you have from the topics in this book. Use AI, learn to write good prompts (questions and commands), and find a nice AI tool you like to use.

Most people have now heard about ChatGPT and its various growing models. Many people are now using it for both play and for work. It's as simple as going to https://chatgpt.com/ and signing up. But there is a long list of other AI models and tools you can use. For images and graphics, Midjourney and Dall-E are amazing tools. Now, things are happening fast so I can't say how long this information will be accurate.For you to stay up to date with AI tools and platforms, my grand tip of the day is to bookmark this website:

https://theresanaiforthat.com/

If you are on a Mac, another app I use and can recommend is Raycast. It gives you a lot of features, tools, and AI models built in right on your Mac. With Raycast, you can just set up Cmd+Space as a shortcut and use AI to ask questions. That's some tips on where to find help. It's now time to move on to practical things.

Register your domain and set up WordPress.

Unless you already have a domain name, it's time to register it, set up hosting, and install WordPress.

So, let us start the building process for your new website. You will typically follow this workflow for many of your future client jobs. Sometimes, a customer may already have a domain name. And sometimes they may already have an old website.

Your job will be to start fresh and build from scratch. Unless the client specifically asks you to re-design an existing website.

If you already have a website, you may want to look over this workflow we will now be following. I have been working with many people that come from Wix, Squarespace, and other platforms. But want to go more professional with their career and build on WordPress with 100% control.

But, if you are new and have no website from before, this will be an important step. To register your own domain and set up a WordPress site. It is totally up to you whether you want this website to be public or not. Maybe you just want to keep it closed as a training project. And you, as the administrator, be the only one who can see it. That's fine. You can use this first website as a "playground" to try things out, test designs, and install various plugins to try out.

So, to start off, we will do the following the coming days:

1. Register a domain of your choice with hosting included (domain name + server space to host the website in one package).
2. Installing WordPress with SSL/HTTPS (automatically).
3. Install a design theme or use a page-builder.

This first step will be to pick a good domain and hosting service. I have one ready for you. And this part will most likely be the most technical for you. But it's not complicated at all. You'll fill out some registration fields and click around to install WordPress. It will be a good practice because you will do the same thing for your future customers.

Especially for simple jobs with customers that don't have a domain or website already. If you keep using the same service as I recommend for you now, you will quickly learn how to use it.

Now, I have to be fair. It is always easier to learn from interactive videos instead of reading things out from a book. But the process I have put in this book is pretty straightforward.

Just keep in mind that you can get way more detailed help from my course platform. Link in the resource section on my website.

Now let's start getting a domain name that you like.

Register your domain name with a hosting package included.

As I mentioned at the beginning of this book, a hosting service can offer both domain registrations and a hosting package in one bundle. And that's what we will be choosing at this time. There's no need to register your domain name in one place and find hosting somewhere else. It's just way more technical.

It's good to get this first step done because the website you build will need a domain name so we can easily find your website and view it in the browser. We also need a server (hosting) space to install WordPress on. Yes, other ways exist to make websites without a domain name connected. But that will be a topic for dinner later.

My first service recommendation for you is Dreamhost. This hosting company has a simple dashboard where you manage all your domains, email accounts, and websites in one place. And installing WordPress is just a few clicks.

Next - Go here: Dreamhost.com

They have good prices, especially in the first year, which makes it affordable to get started. Dreamhost has many services and options. But when you go to their website using the link above, you will come to the correct page for the type of hosting you need.

Down on that page, make sure you select "Shared Starter" or "Shared Unlimited." I strongly recommend **Shared Unlimited**. Because you can set up unlimited websites and email accounts on that package. Plus, the price is low anyway.

When choosing how long you want to register the hosting account, you can go as low as paying per month. But it will always be cheaper to pay for at least one year. The longer you sign up for, the cheaper it will become per month. Usually, paying monthly gets more expensive fast. Make sure you pay attention to this as being charged month by month can quickly become double compared to paying for one year in advance.

1. Choosing your new domain name

So, what will you choose as your domain name for your business or personal freelance brand? When you go to Dreamhost, you can type and search for a domain name of your choice. You will quickly see if it comes up as available.

Let's not spend too much time overthinking that. But you COULD consider your personal name, as long as it's not too long or complicated. Or you could register a completely random and abstract name if it is catchy and short. In the future, your personal brand is more about your story behind it than simply a sexy domain name.

And this is what I did a few years ago. I signed up "JohnMac.pro" (instead of .com).

Picking a simple domain name, for now, is better than pondering deep into a cup of coffee, looking for the right swirl and buff of steam to reveal the utterly perfect and divine name that you were born to use from the dawn of day. Just pick a nice domain name for this training. You can always register a new domain name and connect your website to it later.

When you go to Dreamhost and pick a hosting plan, the domain name will be included free of charge for the first year. When you sign up, you will be asked to choose a domain name at the same time. If you want, there is an option to pick your domain name later. This is possible. But for now, I recommend we move on with the typical workflow you will do for clients later.

2. Installing WordPress

After registering your domain name and setting up your new account, you can log into your Dreamhost dashboard. Be aware that sometimes you have to wait **a few minutes or even hours** before your new domain name is ready, updated worldwide, and be accessible to the public. To test if it's ready, try typing it in the browser. If it's ready, a Dreamhost landing page should come up. This is the default dummy page until you replace it with your new WordPress website.

After you log into your Dreamhost account, you will go to **WordPress** and click **Install WordPress** .

This will take you through the setup process for WordPress and connect it to the domain you have just registered. The next step now, unless Dreamhost already did it, is to activate SSL on the domain and for your website. SSL will give you a secure website like **https://yourdomain.com.** You will see this in the browser URL field. Having SSL and getting HTTPS for a website is now the default setup for all new projects.

Do the words SSL and HTTPS sound scary? Don't worry. These two terms are simple, and you'll learn more about them later. Remember, if in doubt, Dreamhost chat support will guide you or even install SSL for you. But most likely, the WordPress installation process took care of it.

Next, as soon as WordPress has been installed, you can log into your WordPress site from a quick-access button in your Dreamhost dashboard. Or by logging in with the username and password that you chose. The page to log into your new website is the same for all WordPress sites. It will be like "YourDomain.com/ **wp-login.php.**" Sometimes you can also use /login after your domain name.

I just need to point out that some of the links and steps in the Dreamhost dashboard may change over time. As platforms like this usually change and improve things regularly.

3. Changing the design of your website

On every website WordPress gets installed, the design will look the same. You will see one of the latest free WordPress themes installed and activated. This theme will be the look and feel of your website for now until you select a different theme. Or install a premium page builder.

By default, WordPress uses "themes" to give a website a specific design. And there are thousands of free and paid themes. You can have many themes installed on your website. But only one can be active at a time.

The themes are nice and straightforward to use. But as I have mentioned before, I never recommend using a free theme when you build websites. They are too limited and aren't flexible at all. You can't really build anything. And if you intend to make money on building websites, using themes won't work well. Unless you find a client who would be happy with a basic site with just a blog. Just keep in mind for the future that if a client at one point wants to upgrade and change things, you're stuck.

So, for the sake of your learning and professional training on how to build sites in a proper way, we will be using a page-builder instead. But of course, if your budget is low and you want to try things out, test your site with a free theme for now. Play with the WordPress themes gallery and try several of them. No harm in that. Just be aware that some of the "free" themes are not really free as you start using them. Often theme developers want you to upgrade to a paid version of the theme which will have more features. This CAN be totally fine to do. But again, you're limited to the predefined design and functionality of the theme.

Another note about using paid "premium themes" is that they often demand you install a bunch of add-on plugins for their features to work. I don't like that, because you're forced to use various additional plugins you really don't want on the site.

You will find hundreds of free themes in the WordPress settings under Appearance > Themes to play with.

But the best thing now is learning how to set up a website using a proper page builder. And with this book, I will only recommend what I use, so you can copy my workflows and thinking. And to make sure you learn about and adapt to the craft of the pros out there. This is a moment where we don't want to pick a cheap or free too. Because it will limit your income.

With a professional WordPress page builder, you will have A LOT more control to build custom websites. Even close to app-like solutions, by just using WordPress. And with a much higher price value.

When installing a page builder, they sometimes come as regular WordPress themes. And sometimes, it's just a plugin. If it's a plugin, WordPress will often disable the regular themes feature altogether. You will see what I mean when you get to use such a page builder.

We're now at a point in this book where you have two choices:

- Try things out and continue with a free WordPress theme
- Go all in to actually build and design stuff with a professional page-builder for WordPress.

The page-builder I use and will advise you to get is Bricks Builder. It's an investment in your future and the freedom you will have to build what you want.

You can see more at Bricksbuilder.com

If you're not ready for it, you can of course start setting up websites using free themes. But as I mentioned, you are not designing or building anything. You simply have to use a pre-designed and limited WordPress theme.

When starting small and trying things out, you can set up good-looking websites for clients and get paid. But getting your Bricks license will give full design and building control. Another option is Oxygen Builder, which also is well known in the industry. But Bricks is faster, more elegant, and more modern.

Why Bricks Builder?

When you purchase Bricks Builder as a primary building tool, you will earn the cost of purchase back tenfold from your upcoming client jobs. ONE paid job, and you get your investment back. It's a clever purchase because Bricks will be your primary design and website building tool to create what clients want.

The Bricks Builder theme is a modern, clean, and flexible WordPress page builder built on the "VueJS" framework (Whatever). This means that it's fast, lightweight, and quick to work with. And now, you can find a lot of free extensions and resources to build your websites even quicker.

You'll even find websites offering professional and free Bricks templates that you are free to use in your client projects. Again, I'm reminding you how the design job has basically been done for you. It's super-fast to add blog sections, email opt-ins, forms, login modules, and a long list of other included modules that come with Bricks Builder. All within a clean click-and-drag interface.

Bricks is a **VISUAL** website builder, which makes it fast to create pages by using sections, rows, and modules, quickly. Again, this is not something you can do when using a free WordPress theme. Again, using a professional page builder makes it open for you to charge much higher prices for your Web Design work. And still, with no coding involved. The more you play with Bricks or Oxygen as your page-builder, the quicker your income will grow over time.

Consider Oxygen Builder for WordPress

I have mentioned another very effective website builder for WordPress. One that I have used a lot for custom client projects. My last job using Oxygen was a $15,000 custom WordPress website for a client that now pays me monthly to support them.

Oxygen Builder can look more advanced. But it is still a visual drag-and-drop page builder. Though, I think you should know more about some minor technical details around website building before using it. If you are not entirely new to Web Design and know little about structuring a webpage, you could purchase Oxygen Builder and start with that. It's a fantastic investment and a no-brainer if you decide you want to get good at building websites and want full control. I have built some pretty nifty websites using the Oxygen Builder. (still without coding)

The Conclusion

So to recap. Bricks or oxygen should be your only two choices as a primary building tool for websites. Both for yourself and your customers. I use Bricks Builder, and it covers all WordPress website projects I take on. But small and complex jobs.

As we move into the future, there will always be new tools like this. But that is something you will discover as you enter this game.

Before we continue this book to get into how you will get paid from your clients, I want to make sure you're not leaving the process or abandoning your dream at this point.

Since I'm confined to teach and share knowledge through this specific format, a book; I'm pretty limited to how I can teach and train you in the technical side of things. So far, registering a domain name, logging in to your account, and installing WordPress...

That's fine. But how do you continue from now on?

This is where the figure-shit-out mentality should kick in. I don't want to abandon you on the technical side of things. But unless you sign up for one of my courses or try out videos on YouTube, workflows and specifics on Bricks and a website building process will be hard to show you. Even though many of these things are not hard, your learning will accelerate by following how-to videos in a course.

So, don't give up. Stick with it. Play and hack around with stuff, and you'll discover cool things you can do just like I did in the beginning.

If you only start with free WordPress themes, you should easily figure things out. If you go for a Bricks Builder license purchase, there's a never-ending list of YouTube videos already.

The biggest purpose of this book is to train your mind on the PROPER way of starting as a Web Designer. To think like one and give you the steps to begin with enough knowledge and tools to actually start earning your first income from it.

So, let's talk about getting paid.

Getting ready to add tasks and to get paid

Let's focus on opening up the mind to getting paid and setting up the tools to manage your project tasks.

P reparing for a nice money flow is much simpler than the technical setup in the previous one. And I will recommend three different tools you can use to get paid.

I have put some time into this chapter to also touch on the topic of the money-mindset. Because I know, also from my own experience, that being responsible for your own wealth-success can be a huge mountain to climb. Most people are used to bow and say thank you for their fixed monthly payment. The usual, predictable, but flat salary coming from your company.

This will be a change for your fear-based mind now that you will have to define and set your own salary. Then tell your client to pay you. For some, this is not a big deal. But I would say, for most beginners, it's a big deal and a scary first step.

The reason?

Well, how much do you consider yourself to be worth? Can you really ask that customer for $3000 dollars in an invoice with your name on it? What will they think of you? Who do you think you are!?...

Yeah, exactly that last question is the point here. Your self-worth. Which touches on spiritual and existential values many people never focus on. Coming from a society where it's normal and obvious to just do what you're told, turning the table will mess with your mind. And with your feelings.

You will need to consider this when preparing to start charging for your services. Now is the time to gradually start valuing the standards for your craft and what price level it should have. Unless you're already confident and maybe even used to asking for payments from customers.

> Simple but sharp standards and humble confidence work like magic. Your customers will like it. And it will raise your income.

Meditate on this if you need to. Start picturing yourself being a one-man business and online entrepreneur that has skills people will pay you for. Over time, setting prices and sending invoices will feel better and better. And the more confident you get, the fewer problems you will have asking for the right price for your work. Your customers will also ask fewer questions. Customers pay for confidence and skills.

It's essential to ask clients for payment BEFORE the work starts. And this is not to be ashamed of. It's a professional way of working with clients. And it is a commitment and safety for both you and the client. Sometimes I even charge 70% upfront. It all depends on the size of the job, the total price, and the feeling I get from the client. If I'm unsure about their seriousness, I invoice them at least 70%, and sometimes even 100% up front. I can do this because I'm confident in my personality and my skills.

There are two reasons why I put the money mindset and payment setup at this part of the book.

1. To make sure your system for earning money is ready to go

"Hey, I'm currently working on some new creative skills in design, and I'd like to help you guys out with a new website. When I am done, you can decide whether you'd like to pay for my service or not. No obligations..."

YOU are the product that clients want...

2. To make sure you're professionally set up from the start

It's easy to stand out and look good with your freelance and personal branding. Having a simple website, making an AI logo online, and having a simple payment and invoicing system is easy to set up. When these things are in place, customers feel much better sending you money for your services.

It's not hard to sharpen the standards for yourself. It's an easy discipline. And it's simple to find the tools and inspiration online. Walk and talk as a professional. Without being cocky or overdoing it. Just have an elegant, demeaning attitude to your daily life and craftsmanship online. Customers love this. No need to wear a suit or white gloves. Just some nice, simple standards for yourself that signal your branding.

If you wish to create a simple logo and start branding yourself, you can easily make one using tools like Fiverr.com/logomaker or https://looka.com/

Having a good standard in your branding makes it easier and more comfortable to start asking for payment from clients.

So let's make sure you're set up with an invoicing tool early to charge for your Web Design services promptly. We won't overthink it; we'll ensure a smooth start and make sending payment links enjoyable for your clients.

But first, one important thing to consider:

If you are completely new and just starting your career as a Web designer or a creative freelancer working online. You should be prepared to not charge anything for your work in the beginning!

Yes, that's right. It's an easy ticket into the doorstep of the customer. Also, remember that customers pay for what you can deliver. They pay for the confidence in your work, brainpower, and skills. YOU are the product. When starting out, consider just getting a couple of website projects done to have happy customers who recommend you. When starting out and you're fresh in your skills, you can't go wrong with this since you're not asking for money in exchange. And taking on a few simple jobs for free is better than not getting any work at all in the beginning.

But, of course, if you can get paid, that's even better. And that's why we want the invoicing setup ready to go. Let's aim for the stars and focus on getting paid for your first jobs just for the sport of it.

Just keep in mind that the value of 2-3 free projects in the beginning is the clients recommending you further.

So, getting your first potential customers this week can be easier using the following word script below. Reciprocity is a powerful dynamic in sales.

Word Script

For someone that does not have a website, this is a VERY good offer. So aim to look for that type of client first. Next, if you set up a simple site that looks good and works well, I know some clients would feel obligated to give you at least some compensation for your hard work. If you could at least get paid $300 - $500 for a very simple website, do it! It will pay back your investments for the hosting and the purchase of Bricks Builder in a snap. Let's continue. We'll be setting up a neat way to get paid online, and looking good with it at the same time. And then find a nice project and task management tool to keep track of your work.

Two tasks for today

✓ Prepare a nice invoicing tool.
✓ Sign up with Stripe to accept credit card payments.

There are many services and tools to create invoices and do bookkeeping and accounting. For now, I will focus on the invoicing part to make sure your potential client can pay for the first 50% of the job before you start. (Or 70% if you can bargain that.) To have your clients pay you in a smooth way, I will suggest three services I think are good. I have used two of them myself before, so I know how they work. The last tip is more modern and probably what fits you best for now.

- Use Waveapps.com to get invoicing and accounting for free
- Use FreeAgent.com to have invoicing and accounting
- Use Invoice.2go.com for a very modern and slick solution

If I were to choose at this time, I would go for Invoice2Go. They look good, have a modern interface, and a good mobile app.

Setting up an account here is something you will just dive into when you want to focus on it. Bookmark the service you want to try and jump into it later. Let's cover another service I recommend you sign up for. And it's free to register an account.

Setting up a Stripe account

If you have not heard about Stripe, it's the world's leading online credit card payment service. I use them for all my payment integrations. And so do thousands of other businesses, SaaS entrepreneurs, and freelancers. Stripe is available in many countries, so go and check out their signup page if it's available for you as well.

They have a beautiful platform that integrates with almost everything you can imagine. And most likely, Stripe has been the payment processor you have used online or in a mobile app before without even knowing it.

You need a free Stripe.com account to let your customers pay with their credit cards. After setting up your Stripe account, you can log into the invoicing/ accounting service you chose in step one and connect it with Stripe. This way, your customers can click a link in the invoice email from that service and pay you directly in the browser.

Stripe will capture the payment and automatically send it to the bank account you have set up in your Stripe settings when signing up.

Setting up a Stripe account is free, with no monthly cost. The only charge for using Stripe is per payment transaction. Just like with any other online payment platforms. You can't avoid this. It's how they make their business turn. The cost is usually around 2.4% of the transaction being processed. Try using Stripe as much as possible, as PayPal sucks with their clever and tricky fees and terrible platform culture. I have no feelings for PayPal. And you will notice later that in our industry, people with experience do not like PayPal.

It is also a good practice for you to know the basics about Stripe, how it works, and how it integrates with apps, tools, and plugins. Because sooner or later you will come to a point where clients will need your advice in setting it up for their own websites and integrations.

Important Reminder:

As I mentioned earlier, always charge your clients 50% to 70% for the quoted project price in advance before any work you start. When you do, indicate this with a note on your invoice. Something like:

"This is invoice 1/2 at 50% of the price given for your project. Any additional work added during the project time will be added to the final invoice".

Your first customer is just around the corner

Let's get into the mindset of you working for your first Web Design client. It can be family, friends, or connections to someone with a small business.

N ow is the time to plan for and seek out your first customer project. This can be a paid job or a free service to build your reputation and expertise. But let's aim for the goal of getting paid. Even if you say you will offer this for free as a "support project". Because when you finish the project for your client contact, suggest a "pay-what-you-want" arrangement.

Like I said before, reciprocity has a strong presence in human minds. So the emotional need to return the "favor" could present itself as a nice "donation" for your work.

Start early to open up for potential customers. Since you have set up your invoicing system, you are ready to send an invoice with a payment link in case a paid project comes up.

Today's money-making task

✓ Make a list of potential customers.

Doing this work now will help your mind to get into the habit of thinking about clients. I believe that over time, by completing a few jobs, your reputation will sell for you. And new requests for website projects will come in. That's how I have built the lifestyle I have now. Because I always had work coming in, on autopilot. And I still do. So, let's do some brainstorming together. Where could you possibly find your first client web design project?

Let's start with potential paying clients on top. Your first client project could be a local store owner, a friend, or a local sports team. So keep brainstorming using the following ideas of businesses and contacts.

- **A company:** Do you know a CEO, boss, or decision-maker in a small company, locally or online? Contact them with your offer. You could aim for a small company that doesn't even have a website yet (for some reason).

- **A local store:** Do you know the owner or have a friend working at a local store that would need a new website or upgrade an existing one? Pick a store that's not part of a bigger business chain. Because the store owner usually can't decide for the whole company. And those bigger companies have websites already. It's also a project you don't want to take on as your first project.

- **A sports team:** Are you into a sports team or local membership, or do you know anyone with such a membership? Many local sport teams do not have a website yet. Many of them are just relying on Facebook features.

- **A friend's new business:** Do you know anyone that has started a new business or money-making hobby? A dog trainer, coach, financial advisor, spiritual counselor, or similar one-man business?

- **A friend's hobby:** This is the last one to be paid for, but it could be a good reference project for later. Someone you know will have a hobby or particular interest that could benefit from a website.

Be creative, and don't drop ideas just because you picture it couldn't happen. When talking to your contacts, be service-minded and let them know your purpose for this work. This is to grow your network and have more website projects done so you build your reputation and experience.

As soon as you have finished the website, your customer becomes your first promotion channel and advocate for your business. It's the best marketing you can have. Happy customers talk.

Remember that the most important thing is to get your first project, enjoy the work, and level up your experience. The more hours you get in building, the faster and simpler it will be for you to get the next job. Remember that income grows along with experience. The more websites you build, the higher your value and, thus, your price will go up. Write some ideas for potential clients in a table like the one I provided.

Business/Name	What do they do?	Contact

For most beginners, the scariest part is to start presenting and offering your skills to the world. The best advice I can give is this (and you may need to remove some old subconscious programming that's been stuck in you for a long time):

"The customer is NOT always right."

To me, this is some old sales crap that sounds more like "obey and serve whatever the client wants at all costs to get the sale." Bad and fake American-style sales mindset. So delete that from your mind.

No, the client is not always right. We're not obeying clients like servants. And you should not approach a company with your tail between your legs and your hat in your hand. Feeling all shaky and nervous like you were applying for a new job. Nope. You're now the captain of your ship, and you decide whom to work with. You're in a position to offer your services to a business or friend because you want to. You're presenting yourself with confidence and offer them an OPPORTUNITY to work with you. You enter the scene without being cocky of course. But with clarity, confidence, and a slight joyfulness. Of course, for a fresh web designer with no experience in this kind of customer relationship, it can be a bit intimidating. Also, if you're unsure about your capacity and confidence in building what the clients wish for, I would say, this is just part of the learning and process of your growth. To improve communication and be more prepared, make sure you do a quick research about them on the following points before you visit the business or talk to any decision-makers. Just do a quick look-up to have a bit more insight into their business. And figure out what website they have today, if any. Then, see if you can figure out these details as well.

- Where do they have their hosting (if any)?
- How has their current website been built?
- Could you make it better using Bricks or Oxygen Builder?
- What functions could you add to their site to make it more useful?

Word scripts to use with potential clients

Here are a few scripted phrases to use when approaching the business and suggesting your offer for a new website. If they don't want your offer, confidently smile and say thanks. And move on to the next client.

"So I wanted to suggest to you today to build a new website for you. I have a passion for Web Design, and I'm improving my skills and new brand. I'm willing to help you out for a very affordable price. What budget could you set aside for your business to look good online?"

"I'm starting my new freelance business helping people look good online. I want to offer you a brand new website with the most modern and flexible website builder. I'll make it useful for you guys, and you can set the price after I'm done."

"One thing that too many website owners struggle with is working with outdated website systems and themes. If you want something good-looking that you can maintain yourself, I'll be the one to set this up for you. What's your budget to improve your most important online platform?"

Now read through these suggestions a few times and even practice with some friends. Make it natural for you without sounding like a robot. Don't sing it out and over-act like in the Sound of Music. Just consider my suggestion and make it sound like you, with confidence. Tweak it to your tone if you will.

Some administrative tips before you start working with client projects

I will be going into some important scenarios and tips for you to be more prepared for typical client jobs. Again, the biggest growth you can have is to start working with clients, gain experience, and even fail at times. Failing is part of the hero's journey!

Some questions will come up for you during a conversation with a customer and while planning the details for a website project. So here are a few typical questions you may get and that we can cover right now:

If the customer already has a domain and hosting, you can give them the login details to their hosting company's control panel. They can send this to you via email, or post it in one of your project management tools you could add them to. You need these details to work with them and get things done.

If they don't have a website, domain name, or hosting, you will suggest where to set that up. Ask the customer if they will do the domain and hosting registration themselves. And use your own affiliate link to a hosting company like Dreamhost. This will give you a small commission if the client signs up. If not, you can pick the hosting company you are comfortable working with. I still recommend using Dreamhost for the first simple websites you build. Plus, you will be working with the client in a hosting dashboard you are familiar with.

In this process, make it clear to the customer that they will have to pay for their domain and hosting outside of your quoted project price. And think about what we went through in chapter one. Keep it simple for both you and the customer. And picking a domain name is usually easier for a registered business with an established name. If you will be registering domains, hosting, and other services for the client, you will need their credit card details. Which is not always that easy for a customer to just give out. For me, I generally have the trust with my clients and I keep records of various credit cards for them in a safe encrypted format. This way, it's much easier for me to help them again in the future.

Make sure you professionally handle this when handling such information. Make sure you take note of both credit card numbers, date, and CVV number. And don't write this down on a piece of paper. Use a password manager like **1Password** or **LastPass.**

Not all clients will hand you their credit card information, of course. In that case, you will tell them they will receive an email from you with the link to sign up for their domain and hosting themselves.

As the clever Web designer you are, you will sign up for Dreamhost's affiliate program first. Then send your customer your affiliate link and make a few dollars even before you start working. If your customer signs up for a Dreamhost account for one year, you can easily get paid $100 by Dreamhost for that. This is a great start to begin growing your passive income.

If all this information is new to your ears, get my short ebook about recurring and passive income. Make sure you get some essential details on affiliate programs and how you should work smart to grow your passive income.

https://johnmac.pro/affiliate-ebook

While handling this beginning stage of a web design project, make sure you take care of things and make it easy for the customer to say yes. Don't bother them with an overload of technical stuff. Just serve them and make them feel taken care of. If you're challenged, make notes and tell them you're getting back to them about their question or comment. It gives you some time to check on details so you can confidently answer them in the next conversation or follow-up email.

Next, let's talk about email accounts. This is a topic that will come up sooner or later. And for clients that are a bit inexperienced with domains, websites, hosting, and email accounts, guide them to understand what they need. When a customer registers a new domain, it is proper to explain that they should also have an email account on the domain. So when setting up a new email account on the customer's new domain, ask them what email address they would like. For example, "mail@yourdomain.com." Way too many businesses use private emails like Gmail or other weird stuff. This just looks cheap and unprofessional.

When signing up to Dreamhost using the package I explained earlier in this book, you will have email accounts included. If you suggest Dreamhost for a client project, suggest the same package so they can freely create email accounts on the domain as needed. If there are questions you can't answer or you're unsure of the work details, tell them you will look into it and follow up via email with them.

What if I cant do the work?

If the work they ask for is out of your reach, that's totally fine. I recommend being honest about it. Tell them that you have reviewed their request and recommend they move on with a different web designer at this time.

Discovering what type of tasks and technical work you will be doing for a client should come through during the initial or second conversation with them. So before you begin the project, now. now. Often while a project has started and you're catching up with the client, they suddenly get some magical cosmic downloads and get new ideas about new changes to the project.

If this happens, the price SHOULD change. And you just have to review if you can accept the changes and requirements.

Next, let's take a look at how to put a price on your work. The ultimate question all freelancers will ask sooner or later.

How to price and charge for your work

Setting a price and requesting payment can be an unsettling experience initially, primarily because individuals are accustomed to having others determine their worth.

What we will cover in this chapter is going to be an important topic to talk about. Because if we don't, you will most likely sell yourself cheap and feel that all the hours you put into your business and client projects are just not being valued. What you get paid is not what you wanted, and defeat creeps in.

This is a common challenge and happens to most people starting a work-from-home or freelance business. Selling yourself cheap is a typical issue when starting out because you believe your craft is not worth paying for. Another common twisted mindset is the fear of asking for money in exchange for your service in general. Which links back to the topic we touched on in the chapter called "Getting ready to add tasks and to get paid".

For the majority of people, they're used to having a job and getting paid a pre-defined monthly salary. And of course, they only get paid while on duty between 9 and 5 or whatever hours they signed up for. This is an EMPLOYEE'S way of being compensated! Which, for the most part, will stay flat and not grow over time. Except for one glorious day when you may have been able to raise your salary $3 more per hour.

There are smarter ways to work to make a living. Having a job is certainly not the only source of income. Instead, you can have multiple income streams by offering your qualities and skills. And YOU get to set the prices. Plus, you will have greater freedom. But now the challenge comes. How do you set the prices?

As a web designer, how much can you, and should you charge for making websites as a beginner? Thank you for asking that question; it's a good one!

The short answer: You should get paid for your level of experience and knowledge, and with a minimum compensation for your actual technical and creative work.

The broader your skill level to support your customers in various ways, the more valuable you become to them. The more you can solve problems, give answers to their questions, and find solutions, the higher your hourly rate. The faster you learn, the sooner your project prices can grow. The more you earn, the fewer jobs you need to make a good living. And before you know it, your energy, happiness, and feeling of freedom and control will fall upon you. And there will be nothing but white puffy clouds in the sky at all times.

Maybe you'll become good at graphic design, copy editing, image editing, SEO, or other magic tricks that could help the client. And if you have crafty skills, the client will most likely choose to stick with you instead of searching for others. Now you're moving into a landscape of client VIP zone and work abundance, and you can start picking the most exciting jobs.

First, let's look at the typical rates freelancers and Digital Nomads get paid worldwide. This will be a good starting point and a nice overview of where to position yourself in the pricing scale as a beginner hacker.

I did some research so you can look at these sources yourself. I found one reference from the well-known accounting and invoicing service called Freshbooks: "How much do Web Designers charge". And they seem to keep this article updated.

There would be a big difference in hourly rate if you were back to being employed as a Web Designer compared to becoming your own boss. And by having a look online, here's the comparison. Jot this one down:

Stuck-in-office employee: $28 - $40 hourly rate
Being your own damn boss: $75 - $130 hourly rate (typical)

Luckily, you're in the last group. Because sensible people spend time doing what they love, right? Now, as a beginner, I would suggest going a little lower on the hourly rate for now. Like $35 - $65 per hour.

Later, if you decide to just become freakin' awesome and a must-have freelancer with build-in charm, charisma, and high-end cyber skills, you can even go up into the $250 range for some projects. Then you can wear sunglasses, have a slick haircut, smell good, and become as irresistibly handsome as the author of this book. All while you are working from the sky, on a beach, or the top of a mountain with a Starlink by your side.

Next, here are some factors that come into play when deciding on a price for a client. These are important metrics I relate to when determining the time needed and what quote I give to the client.

- Your experience level
- Type of business or client you will be working with
- Where in the world the client comes from
- Type of work to be done
- If the clients keep coming back for more work

I'll quickly cover each point in this list right now.

Your experience level has to start somewhere. The training you get from this book lays the foundation for your self-education from now. And as you build

66

more websites, your skills will improve, which equals better compensation. And it's up to you to choose how quickly you wish to level up by playing with it, testing things, and just build cool stuff even if nobody requested it. Even as a beginner, you will already know more than most of your future clients. Soon, the more you know, the greater your confidence. And your clients won't flinch when you set hourly and project-based rates for their requests.

Quotes for a project will also be related to and reflect the **type of business** you're doing the work for. Will you take on a small job for a friend or a local sports club? Or did you score a bigger job for a company that can afford to pay what you deserve? Keep this in mind for the future. Don't just aim for the small fish just because it's easy and feels more comfortable. Aim for the whales.

Where in the world the client comes from has a big impact on what you can charge. For example, if you live in the U.S. or a European country and get connected with a client from Romania or Africa, you most likely won't take that job. They won't be able to pay what you're worth because the income and currency level is much lower. Clients from some parts of the world simply can't afford you. Unless you're doing a Mr. Nice Guy charity project. I have personally received a few requests from Africa at price levels that made me laugh.

The type of work your client requests will determine the complexity, time needed, and thus, the cost of the project. For example, I always set a different price for administrative, easygoing work meetings. Minor technical support usually has a lower rate, while more advanced custom work in WordPress goes higher. Design changes, various integrations, and domain work will usually have a higher price because it is more time-consuming and complex tasks. It is simply worth more. It's harder for the client to find good people to do this because fewer people have those skills. For me, I have accumulated so much knowledge and insight into WordPress, themes, plugins, custom integrations, and design work that I have, over time, gained a reputation for it. That's why many clients don't want to start over, seeking out someone who knows their stuff. The same is true for you.

> Raising your quality of work, knowledge, and skills will make you lucrative. And more clients will fight for your availability.

But then, over time, I would lower the price again **if the client keeps coming back.** I do this to show appreciation for their trust. And to make working with me more affordable. That makes the clients happy, and it will establish a longer customer relationship. This always works. And it makes me feel safe knowing I will have regular clients who keep returning to me for more work. Project after project. Updates after updates.

Usually, it will be easier to keep working for the same client in the long run instead of establishing an understanding of new clients and project details over and over. New jobs are also fun, of course. But you will feel more confident in your business by having at least a few regular clients. This shows they like you, and it gives predictable income in your business.

How to estimate a price for the job

First, keep your new insights from the previous section in mind. Then review and consider the amount of work to be done for a project. I usually estimate my prices in the following way:

- One fixed price based on the client's project description.
- Then an hour-based rate for any changes or added work.

By giving the client a fixed and flat project price for the job, your customer will feel more secure with the project. They feel safer knowing what they will have to pay. If you told the client after reviewing their request:

"Nice, this looks good, I can do this, and we can start when you are ready. My hourly rate is $75 per hour, thank you"

In the next moment you may observe your client's face turn pale. Then they will ask how many hours this will take. And if you reply something like;

"We'll just have to see how it goes."

-You won't get the job. Because the client is not interested in a surprise bill at the end.

Your ability to estimate a fixed price comes with experience because you know what you're up to and roughly how long the various tasks will take. As a beginner, you won't know. So, what I will add here as guidelines are some beginner price points for usual tasks you will be doing when working on typical WordPress projects.

In this table below, I'm simply suggesting some prices I think you should charge as a beginner web designer. Remember that you should complete your work effectively but properly. This ensures you're not spending more time than necessary. This will raise your hourly rate. The quicker you do things, the more you will be left with per hour, yes?

What you should be paid for is a mix between skill level, complexity, and time spent.

And everything takes time! For example, when registering a domain for a client, a task many customers don't know how to do: Charge for one hour, even though this shouldn't take more than 30 min. Keep in mind that your work starts in the moment you receive an email or phone call from a client. Because reading, evaluating, and checking up on things takes TIME. You may have to do some research, respond to the client, wait for a reply, then do the actual work.

At the same time, registering a domain name won't take two hours, either! So don't be dirty and add hours for something that actually takes 30 minutes for someone who knows what they do. Your clients will not pay you for time spent as a beginner.

Next, find the below table as a starting point and reference for future work.

Registering a domain	Charge a minimum of 1 hour to cover all conversations, emailing, the task itself, and the follow-up in the end:
Installing WordPress, Bricks, or other builder	1 Hour - rate at $65
Building pages, contact forms, adding video, integrating plugins	Hourly rate at $65
Administrative work that should be considered pa work	Hourly rate at $35
Adding content to the website	Hourly rate at $45
For a complete website project: With a simple design where the client can make a ONE time simple adjustments on a predefined design.	Fixed prices between $990 - $2000. Beginner level quote. Depends a lot on the end result of course.
Registering a new domain + installing WordPress + setting up Bricks basic install + adding 6 pages to the website + adding the clients basic content on six pages + adding one contact form on one page.	

By being clear with what you get, and no changes are made along the way, you can do a simple job quickly. And if you're able to track the time spent on the job, you will quickly find how much per hour you're left with for the project.

When it comes to the copy (text) and images, the content from the client has to be ready for you. It often happens that a client wants a website, but they barely have either text, logo, or images. If they ask you to help write and provide content, add an x-amount of hours to the project!

But if the website content is ready, and you do such a job in 9 hours, you're close to a $100 hourly rate. Good work!

Some tasks do not require a Web Designer's expertise, such as adding content to the website and tweaking some text. Basically, this is something the client can do themselves. So I usually lower the rate since the value of the work is lower. That also makes it more tempting for the client to have you do it because you make it more affordable for them to have you do it.

Simple rules for setting a prices

Let's recap. If you're doing smaller tasks, charge by your hourly rate. If you're doing many tasks that end up being a complete job, set a fixed price. Just make sure you get ALL the details and expectations from your client. Make sure you outline the expected work to be done in a one or two-page project description where the price is included.

One more important note: Do not allow the client to start adding or making changes to the project without discussing a new price level. Some clients will ruthlessly suck you dry for all the time and energy they can get out of you AFTER a price has been given for the project. So, as I have mentioned before: The client is NOT always right!

Claim your space, demand respect for your profession and time, and set boundaries. It's a reason your client is coming to you in the first place. If you see sneaky changes starting to tick into your email inbox, be quick at notifying your client that you will make note of these changes. And that the added workhorse for the changes requested will be added to the last invoice.

Again, everything comes down to you acquiring experience. It's not about a fancy school degree or formal education. It's just about your personal transformation into a knowledgeable consultant and "web technician" who knows their stuff. Something you'll learn quickly when playing with WordPress, taking courses, watching YouTube videos, and reading blog posts. While you at the same time enjoy building stuff.

Tweak your mind to allow you to receive

I'm adding a short segment as the last part of this chapter to help reduce the fear of getting paid. Because it is a widespread problem. I remember the feeling many years ago before I understood my worth and expertise:

The fear of asking for a fair price.

Beginners are afraid of losing the project if they ask for too much. Beginners are worried they seem greedy and needy. Beginners feel they don't deserve asking for a proper price. But the thing is, now it's time for YOU to set your hourly rate and claim your worth from the craft and service you will deliver. If you have good intentions as part of your personality, and you truly want to deliver support and quality work, then you certainly deserve to get paid accordingly.

I had a conversation with a freelancer working online the other day. She mentioned a time when a couple of her friends that had started online said;

"Sometimes I feel ashamed of receiving such a   good income for the amount of work I do..."

I'm not surprised. Setting your own prices and receiving good payments reflecting what you are worth can be overwhelming for people. And it's especially a common theme for people who come from troubled backgrounds where money struggles have been an issue. And that is exactly what has been my story.

This is simply bad programming from our past. And I wanted to make sure I mentioned this in my book. Not just because of my own terrible money-education. But because I have also met and know many people who try to create a better   life and new income for themselves. Many of them are individuals that have had some of the same background as I have had. And they struggle with the same self-confidence on the topic of money. This is a rough learning. And it can be a real struggle for some people to even be successful no matter how skilled and authentic they are. Blocking your own success, growth, and wealth is a very common issue. And you should at least have an awareness around this in case you would experience strong feelings around the topic of money and wealth.

For me, I had a rough childhood with my mother constantly struggling with money. So in my earlier years, money was always an issue. It became a negative mother-karma that I was dragging into the future. It took time to heal it and become "worthy." And to not see money as something bad, negative, or stressful. But as an energy form that follows my inner feelings about abundance and well-being.

Now it's time for you to get used to it. You're worth astronomically more than you "think." For great work delivered with a professionally communicated service to your clients, you're worth more than you expect. Relax and find your strength. Know that you will be growing a new business where you decide your value. Start loving the feeling of receiving payments. And enjoy good fortune in the spirit of the quality human being that you are.

Start today, be your own boss, and decide to up your skill level so you can award yourself a couple of raises in hourly rates SEVERAL times a year!

Setting up your Project Management System

Being productive brings confidence. And it's lucrative. Let's pick a project management system and to-do app.

This is an important step. And you will love a proper workflow because feeling organized brings an inner state of tidiness and being in control. If you can have that in your work, you will enjoy it more. Another good thing about an organized workflow is that your productivity will increase. This means you spend less time, work is completed faster, and your hourly rate will increase.

If you get paid $200 for a task and spend 1 hour on it, you're doing really well. If you're a disorganized mess and spend 6 hours on it, it's not fun. Your payment will be $33 per hour instead of $200. Of course, in the beginning, things will take more time until you get a good grip of typical tasks and learn techniques around building websites.

To have a productive and meaningful workflow, we need a meaningful to-do app. Or better, a solid Project Management System. It doesn't have to be advanced. And I recommend you don't go overboard with this. Keep it simple, but with features to make the work productive and in a good flow.

Working with proper software is far better than trying to make things organized in Word or Notepad. And you will NOT use Post-it notes on your wall or stuff like MS Excel. Working like this becomes a mess. Train your mind early to get into the habit of using proper tools. Use cloud-based apps so that your work gets synced online into a safe space. This is kind of important, because what if you have several devices? What if you lose your computer? What if you want to share your work with someone remote, like, let's say as remote as Tittybong in Australia. (Yes, it's a real place).

You'll love clicking checkboxes and seeing the outline details of the process from start to finish. It will be easier to modify the process and the checklists. And you get to keep the history of each task, so it's easier to go back in time to check on things if need be. You will feel in more control, and adding new tasks as you start working with a client will be easier.

Another reason to use cloud-based apps or online services with a web browser interface is to access your work from any computer. You can also stay up to date from your mobile phone, which keeps you notified of changes. And you can quickly jump in to look over what projects and tasks you have going while sitting on your favorite café getting new ideas about life, projects, and the future.

It's rewarding to have a professional level of organized workflow for your projects. You make fewer mistakes, and you won't lose track of progress and notes. Over time, your clients will notice your manners and personal discipline. They will respect you for it. They see and feel they are working with someone organized, with high standards, authenticity, and trustworthiness.

You know, the opposite of a politician.

So, to avoid creating a chaotic and unprofessional work environment for yourself, now could be a good time to make it a smooth ride instead. You don't have to stop reading in this very moment. But in the process of putting your learning together and moving on step by step, I recommend deciding on a tool before you start working on a project.

Now, since there are thousands of apps out there, I will suggest a few that are well known. I know them because I have been using them myself. Currently, at the time of writing this book, my team and I are using Basecamp. But here are 4 options you can decide on.

- Basecamp.com - Well known in the industry and easy to use. I believe they also have a free account option now for freelancers.
- Trello.com - Well known and acts as a board with cards in columns. Trello has existed for a long time. If you like column layouts and cards as projects and/or tasks, try out Trello.
- Plutio.com - A complete CRM and project management app. I used Plutio before. I had all my projects, customers, and invoicing here.
- TickTick.com - Fast multi-platform app I use every day. This is a task manager app. But you can also organize projects in many ways.

Remember, I can only suggest a few apps that I know are good. But I recommend that you try out different apps and services yourself so you can get a feel for what you like. We all visualize differently when we think and mentally view project layouts and task structures. And all these apps will give you different ways of setting up projects.

All my recommendations here have good mobile apps, which I recommend you keep in mind. It's nice to be able to view your work on the go and see comments from clients if you later give them access to join one specific project.

If you want to go for some free options, there's a bunch of options there as well. One well-known app is Notion, which most people in the industry know about. Free to use, and you can keep track of tasks in a note or document-like style.

Use well-established online services

There are endless other online services and apps for Mac, Windows, and mobile. Whatever you choose, pick a well-established solution so you won't lose your data after a few months of use in case the company or platform disappears. I always recommend that you pick a service with an iPhone or Android app to stay updated on the go.

In my private coaching with people like you, I also teach how to get started working with a virtual team. That's when it will be essential to have a good platform to mingle, share cat videos, drink coffee, and talk about your office desk flowers. Oh, and keep projects and tasks structured, of course.

So yeah, you may come to a point where you get so much work coming in that you want to consider having one or two people on a virtual team to help with simple tasks. The project management apps I mentioned all have team chat built in.

And of course, to do client calls, the most stable solution I use is still Zoom. I don't fully trust the company for privacy reasons. I know most people don't even consider this topic or even reflect on privacy at all. But that's because they don't really know how things work and what's actually happening behind the scenes. No matter how many scandals that have waved over this planet in the recent years.

So as a last tip on this -keep privacy, encryption, and security in mind instead of just being a blank-slated sheep chewing grass. You have some choices.

Gather the tools of the trade to be productive

Become a productivity expert with effective workflows and fun tools. In this chapter, I'll share more tips for great apps you might need.

When you start doing work on your computer and have a business online, there are a few tools, services, and apps that you will need. I have worked with and tried a lot of different tools and services. There's just an unbelievable amount of software out there in the app jungle. And most of them are crap to work with.

It's easy to get lost in the candy store of apps and software. Not an uncommon habit of people working online. The shiny object syndrome is easy to fall into like other similar things to get hooked in. So with this note, I advise that you stay disciplined and try to stick with software you feel good about.

Productivity is a choice, and you need to be mindful of it. With the right tools, it makes it easier and more fun.

For my part, since I like to focus on workflows, productivity, and software, I like to stay updated with what's out there. And how new software and apps can possibly improve my work. I look for two positive side effects when switching apps:

- It would have to actually improve my workflows.
- Using the software makes me enjoy my work more.

Since I'm part designer and love UX, beautiful interfaces, and form, I need an app that is enjoyable to use. I cramp up and hiss like a cat if I come across tools that look hideous or have no workflows logic at all. Choose what brings joy in your work. But also works well with your mind and way of thinking.

After you have chosen your primary Project Management System, it won't be covering every scenario for the necessary tools we work online. We have different tasks when working creatively online. So having various apps and software is just necessary. Again, to get you started fast, I will suggest a few other tools that are well-known and part of my workflow. Some I use often, some are just apps I need now and then.

The creative craftsman's great bundle of tools

You may have noticed that most entrepreneurs and self-employed in the creative and media business world are Mac users. There is a reason for that. So many of the apps I recommend will be Mac-only. I left the Windows "Swiss cheese" platform many years ago. But if you're a Windows user, there's nothing hindering you from doing great work. You may just have a different choice of software before you. But everything you need is available, with both free and paid options.

Many of the tools I recommend here are platform-independent. I have outlined this list of tools grouped by area or type of work. When it's platform-independent, it means you can also use it on Windows, and even Linux at times. If a software is browser-based, you can use it on any computer that has an Internet connection and a modern browser.

I should mention one important note here. If you happen to be a Linux user, it's usually not recommended for Web Designers. This is because Linux just doesn't have the same type of platform, user interface rendering, and tools available for what you will need in your work. What you see on a Linux computer and in the Linux web browser will look different on a Mac and Windows computer.

So whatever you create and think looks good on Linux will suddenly NOT look the same for the rest of the world. So it's a bad idea. Very few consumers are Linux users and will never be Linux users.

Choice of web browsers

Are you one of those thinking there is only one web browser on this planet? Ah, no. And we're all happy that it's not. There are many web browsers besides Internet Explorer (or was it Explorer...?) Maybe it's called Edge now. Whatever, we don't use that one. Instead, I will make a list of browsers you want to consider so you can become enlightened on this topic as well. You may come to a point where explaining this to clients can become necessary also. And in regards to your work as a web designer, it will be important to check your website builds in various projects to see how it compares.

Different brands of web browsers have a way of rendering web pages differently.

Brave browser - An excellent open-source browser that focuses on privacy and speed. It's loading websites faster than Chrome and Safari. Regular Chrome extensions still work in the Brave browser. I'm putting this one on top because it's my top choice. This browser is stripped of the nasty telemetry and tracking that Chrome from Google is doing. Research it, and you'll stop chewing grass. https://brave.com/

Arc Browser - I know and modern browser from The Browser Company. This one is also still Chrome-based, which means that it's using the Chrome engine in the background. But has been modified and built upon. Arc has a different interface and is focused on increasing workflows and productivity. Chrome extensions also work on Arc - https://arc.net/

Firefox - The new Firefox from Mozilla is going the same way regarding privacy. It's a good browser with a lot of good extensions. I recommend Firefox Developer Edition, just so that you have some extra features when you're ready to use them:
https://www.mozilla.org

Chrome - The second browser on the list. You would need Brave or Chrome installed because your online tools and apps need a Chrome-based browser to function. Just know that Google owns Chrome, and they don't give a shit about tracking you. (Use Chrome and install the DuckDuckGo Privacy Essentials, at least).
https://www.google.com/chrome/

Edge - Edge, hm... is this the one from Microsoft? Never tried it. Let's move on.

Edge?... pff, this is not the browser you are looking for

Min Browser - This is another tiny, open-source, and free browser that I think has been made for developers and conscious users. It's very lightweight and has options to block tracking and JS files completely. I use it at times for my local development and to test websites for mobile view. It's also a privacy- and a security-focused browser with a strict policy on loading scripts. It's also very stripped down and won't install typical Chrome-based extensions.
https://minbrowser.org/

For my part, I never use Chrome. I use Brave, Safari, Firefox, and Min Browser. I switch between them at times to see websites in different browsers and make sure they all render the same layout and details.

Password managers (You will need one)

1Password.com (Multi-platform, free and paid) - The top password manager app for Mac and Windows. Plus others. A very slick app where you can log into websites automatically with a keyboard shortcut. It's one of the most well-known password managers out there.

LastPass.com (Mac/Win, paid) - Another good and well-known password manager I have used before.

Images and graphics work

Acorn (https://flyingmeat.com/acorn/) (Mac, paid) - A low-cost but great replacement for Photoshop. I left Adobe many years ago as they have way too heavy apps and with a constant telemetry to Adobe servers. They are overpriced and overrated.

Canva.com (online, free, and paid) - The tool many people use to create banners, social media posts, logos, and other graphics for print and online use. I use it for my book covers, banners, and YouTube video thumbnails.

GIMP.org - A free Photoshop replacement app that started as a Linux app years ago. A good one. You can use Gimp for Mac and Windows, also.

Coding, development, and FTP

I'm adding this section just as a service to you. You won't need to deal with any coding for now. But if you get to a point where this could be fun and you want to learn, here are a few good resources.

Nova.app (Mac) - Very slick, fast, and well-built code editor for Mac supporting various coding languages and packages (Geeky stuff).

Windsurf (Codeium.com) - A new code editor that's modeled out from VSCode from Microsoft. It has built-in AI chat and code editing with their "Cascade" feature. Very powerful editor to use for simple to advanced coding projects.

Visual Studio Code (Visualstudio.com) (VSCode) - A well-known code editor from Microsoft. Free and open source. You can get a massive amount of extensions and plugins to change the look of the editor and support various coding languages and other tools.

SublimeText.com (Mac, Win) - A free and elegant code editor in case you want to play with that or come to a point where you need one. It also supports theme styling and gives you access to a long list of extensions and language support.

Transmit FTP (Panic.com) (Mac) - Sometimes, we need to upload files to a server. To do that, we use a File Transport Protocol (FTP) app. Though, usually, this won't be necessary for your work.

FileZilla FTP (filezilla-project.org) (Mac, Win) - Another well-known and open-source FTP program, free to download for Mac and Windows. Sometimes, there may be situations where logging into a server and browsing the files for a website is necessary. That's when we use an FTP app.

VPN services for security

You know how crazy the world is when it comes to the Internet and security. So I want to mention a few VPN services. Because you have a responsibility to stay secure with your Internet connection when working with clients and their projects. Especially if you work in cafés and other public spaces.

Using a VPN will encrypt your Internet connection so the person on the next table can't snoop on the Internet traffic you have going in and out from your computer. A VPN should in general be used, as it hides all your Internet activity from your ISP's (Internet Service Providers).

Windscribe.com - My primary choice of VPN service. They also have a no-log policy in their privacy statement and offer a good ad-blocker in the browser extension.

Surfshark.com - A fairly new service on the web. Cool guys with a no-log policy in their business. We like that. Let's hope they keep it.

ProtonVPN.com - A well-known service from the guys creating ProtonMail. They have good apps for Mac and Windows. And if you want to be fully private, you can sign up and pay with crypto, like Bitcoin.

Other useful utilities

CashNotify.com - (Mac, Win) - A slick app giving you instant notifications of incoming payments and updates on your payouts to your bank accounts from Stripe and PayPal.

Reader (Readwise.io/read) (Browser + mobile apps) - To collect your favorite articles online and save them forever. Free and paid. I use it every day to save and read articles I find. You can also forward interesting emails to Reader to view them later. (Click Reader on this website)

Zoom.com (Mac, Win) - The preferred method for video calls and screen sharing with clients. The free version holds meetings up to 40 minutes, and the paid version is unlimited. It can be worth paying for you to host longer calls so you won't get interrupted during your client meetings.

TripMode.ch (Mac, Win) - A must-have app for people like you and me. TripMode controls your data flow when using a hotspot to connect your computer to 4G/5G while on the go. Nothing is worse than having limited data and suddenly you run out because Dropbox or a YouTube video playing in 4K sucked your data plan dry.

Calendly.com - Online meeting scheduling calendar. It integrates with your Google and iCloud calendars, and you can connect it with Zoom. When people book a time with you, a Zoom link for the video call will be sent to the attendee.

Tidycal.com - An almost better alternative to Calendly. And a much cheaper option. It's what I use for all my meeting calendars for clients and customers to schedule calls with me. Be smart, and go to Appsumo to get a lifetime deal.

Craft.do - (free and paid) - Awesome notes and documentation tool. It is beautifully made and platform-independent. I use it for a lot of my work. And also for YouTube film production now. It won the Apple design award previously and is well-known for its beautiful UI.

Team chat and communication

Slack.com (free) - The world's favorite team chat app where we use #channels to group conversations and topics. Just note that it can get noisy and crowded if you join other accounts for other teams, like support teams or services that offer Slack channel access.

Telegram.org (free)- Open-source messenger app for all platforms. Famous for its security (if you use it the right way) and lightweight app. You can also create groups and channels with this app. Supports fast file transfers up to 2GB (higher for paid accounts). Telegram is a good option since you can now organize more content inside folders. And you get installs for Mac, Windows, and Linux.

Note - all the productivity project management apps I have suggested have built-in chat options for your team. So maybe you won't need apps like Slack or Telegram.

Design tools to plan and visualize a website

Sometimes, for bigger jobs, you may want to plan out, sketch, and visualize a website project before actually building it. There are a few tools you can use for this job.

Excalidraw.com - (Free and paid) Awesome simple mind mapping and sketching whiteboard to plan your sitemaps, page layout, and other website content. I use Excalidraw every day in my work to plan, visualize, and organize.

Miro.com - Plan, structure, and mind-map a website project. Well-known and feature-rich platform and tool for content planning.

Figma.com (Recommended) - Professional design sketching, planning, and collaboration tool. Free to use, but you can also pay for collaboration access and more project space when needed.

With this quick-start collection of apps and services, it will be simpler to pick one for the job you need. In the next chapter, I want to help you further by talking about WordPress plugins. I will share a list of recommended plugins and some critical insights you need to remember regarding using plugins in general.

There are certainly a huge list of other software and services you may want to consider. What I use may not be the best for you. It depends on personal preference.

I like to stay up to date with appsumo.com to see what quality software I could be getting on lifetime deals. I have bought (too much) here probably. But also secured several premium lifetime deals so I never have to pay again for those apps. It can save you a lot of money.

Recommended WordPress Plugins and Other Resources

Here are some insights and tips so you can install and use quality plugins safely.

L et's look into some typical WordPress plugins and other resources. Because you will always need plugins for your client projects sooner or later. Plugins are what we install to "plug in" fancy features and necessary functionality on a WordPress website.

Having a list of go-to plugins that you know and trust is a good idea. It makes it faster for you to plan and build client sites. Because you know what you need to install as soon as the client mentions their requirements for the build. I don't necessarily recommend downloading plugins and keeping them on your computer because they keep updating the versions so fast that your saved plugin zip files will be outdated within a couple of weeks.

Though I do it, because sometimes I also work offline with a local server app. Then, as soon as I have completed enough work, I upload the site to a server online, and bulk update all the plugins to the latest version.

Instead, keep the links to the WordPress.org resource or developers' download pages. Or make a list of names for the go-to plugins you will use most of the time. As you keep learning more and discover new and better plugins, you will most likely switch out and use the better ones as you discover them.

An exception would be when you purchase premium plugins. It's a good idea to download and keep those plugins saved, including your license keys.

What are WordPress plugins?

Plugins in WordPress are just like apps on your mobile phone. You are looking for more functions and features, so you install apps. Plugins quickly and easily expand the features on a WordPress site without the need for coding. And this is what I meant in the beginning of the book. What you need to build advanced websites has most likely already been built by developers.

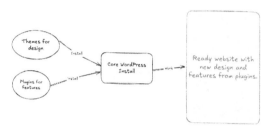

So plugins are one of the main reasons you can build websites without the need for a programmer. There is no reason to reinvent the wheel and recreate what many others have already created as a plugin. Soon or later, when you start building websites for clients, they will most likely have some requirements for both design and functionality. And here are some of the typical features your clients will ask you for.

- A contact form with specific fields, checkboxes, and choices.
- A checkout functionality for credit card payments.
- Custom image galleries.
- Membership systems.
- Instagram feeds on web pages.
- Social sharing buttons.
- Video integrations.
- eCommerce features to have an online store.
- Community plugins.
- User login and authentication.

Do all these fancy and advanced features sound scary to you? Does it look impossible to build features like this? Well, my friend, there is no reason to turn pale. By the grace of developers and coders, somebody has already built what you need for your next client website project. And all those features I just listed above are available for you to simply install and set up using a plugin.

Like with apps and other software, there are thousands of plugins out there. And when you install them, the new features will magically be activated on the website you are building. Usually, there will be a few things to set up to make it all ready. But often, it's just like a "plugin-and-play" installation.

You will quickly see that you can easily get lost in the plugins jungle. Unless you are guided, you will get overwhelmed. And it's way too easy to install the wrong plugins. Ones that are poorly coded, have missing features, or simply not maintained. If the creators and developers of a particular plugin have stopped it, that will become a problem in the future.

When you log into your WordPress website, go to the Plugins page in the navigation. By peeking into this world, you will see the insane amount of plugins. Over the years, I have developed a "feel" for what plugins are good. And those who don't feel right or look bad. Sometimes we have to try and test various plugins. But over time I grew a long list of free and premium (paid) plugins that I always use for various projects.

Knowing what plugins to use will speed up your website workflow. And I am sharing these insights to help you start with a good list of recommended plugins. But first, some critical notes.

Important plugin knowledge

Don't just pick the first plugin in a WordPress or Google plugin search. Start with the WordPress plugins page. When researching, look for well-maintained and high-rated plugins. Check the plugin's last update date, which is usually in the right sidebar. Choose a lightweight plugin that's not too over-complicated, as some can become too big and heavy for your website project.

After installing plugins on a WordPress website, the load time increases due to the scripts and CSS files loaded from the plugins. We only want to install plugins for the necessary features to avoid such scenarios where clients install malicious plugins that drain the site's performance or cause server crashes or hacks.

Also, know that both the Bricks and Oxygen website builders already have a lot of built-in modules and functionality. This can reduce the amount of plugins you need to install. If you will be working on one of these page builders, I suggest keeping this in mind before you start looking for a plugin.

Only download plugins from WordPress.org or the developer's website

This is an important insight to make a note of. When you search for plugins, the first option should be within your WordPress admin or WordPress.org plugin pages. (It's the same as searching within your WordPress Plugins page.)

Never search online and download a plugin from some random website, except for prominent professional creators and developer websites.

If I share any plugin resources with you, notice that they are either linked straight from WordPress.org or the developer's websites where they originate. I would never ask you to download plugins for Dropbox or any other source. So keep that in mind for the future.

There is an abundance of top-quality WordPress plugins sold from developer websites. One example site I can recommend is WPManageninja.com. They produce some advanced and high-quality plugins you may want to consider in the future. I have bought a few from them. So in this case, I just log in to my account and download my purchased plugins from their website.

For many premium plugins, you may first try a free version. Many developers offer this. And you may find the free version in the WordPress "repository," as we call it (the plugins page inside your WordPress). If you like it and want to upgrade with the paid functionalities, go and buy the plugin from their website and download it from there.

You don't want to download plugins from other random sources because of security. Plugin zip files can be modified and changed. And cause security issues on your websites. This could be a disaster, and you don't want that for client websites or your reputation.

This chapter should have now made you more ready to deal with plugins. It's not a complicated or scary topic. You just need to get this basic knowledge about how it works and where to find good plugins.

A tip: I blend the use of free and paid premium plugins all the time. Free plugins are fine, but we often want more fancy features for a website. So, I buy the premium versions. Purchasing paid quality plugins will usually give you one year of updates unless it's a one-time purchase.

If you purchase a premium plugin for a client project, bake it into the price you give the client. If it's a yearly license for the plugin, get the client to purchase it. First, check if the plugin developers have an affiliate program. Sign up and give the link to your client so they can purchase this plugin using your affiliate link.

That was today's abundance tip. You're welcome.

Starting Your First Project For a Client

Time to enjoy the process by starting a client project in a good way, with a proper workflow and a system that gives you control.

C an you picture yourself with a laptop, a cup of coffee, and a cat sleeping on your desk, while smacking up some websites and soon getting paid for it? Back in the days while living in a small apartment in Norway, that was my typical workday. Of course, the cat preferred to sleep on the keyboard.

When I started learning web design, I was a complete beginner with no teacher. For the most part, I have been my own teacher. Also my own coach and motivator. One thing I have been good at is making sure I find constant inspiration and motivation that fuels my fire of desire!

And I have friends who have done the same. I know many self-taught and skilled freelancers who valued their freedom over a flat and dull lifestyle they had no passion for. They quit being "normal" and decided to go their own way. Which is not always accepted and favored by family and friends around you. Something you should be aware of. Societies' simple standards and those who come from Normalville favor and celebrate those who do what everybody else is doing. Stay with the flock, chew grass, and don't be so different.

Well, if you want to do great things in life, you have to step out of the line and walk in the other direction. The most important thing is your current mindset to make this happen. I want you to picture the sound of your keyboard, the smell of coffee, and the work on your screen. Start imagining payments coming in after sending your first invoice to a client. And let that be the motivation to enjoy a new income stream that can grow higher than a normal salary. And not just one income stream. But you have the option to create several of them.

I remember many years ago back in Norway, when I was one of the first enjoying a life of café-surfing while others were stuck at their jobs. Many times people grinned, smiled, and laughed, thinking I was just a computer nerd without a job. Later they discovered my photos on Instagram and YouTube videos and began to see a different lifestyle. Slowly, their smirks dried out, and the crowd turned silent. Some even unfollowed me. I'm not sad.

The time has now come for you to put life force into a personal transformation so that you can thrive from having decided your own destiny and lifestyle. We become what we think. And while we are at it, chew on this one.

Seeing is not believing.
Believing is seeing.
Thoughts come before
reality creation.

Preparing for the new client job

Let's move on. It's time to prepare for a client conversation about their new website. And to understand more of what the client wants from us, we need to ask questions they never thought about. I will share some typical questions I ask new clients when doing a Zoom call or in-person meeting.

Copy these questions into your notes app for you to use later. We usually go through the same questions for most new client projects.

Each client conversation is different. And all projects have different scopes. But there are a few general items on the list you will touch on for each job. Here are the questions I usually ask.

- Do you already have a website?
- Are you using WordPress or something else?
- Where do you have your domain and hosting?
- Could you send me 2-3 links to websites that you like? (to understand more of what kind of design and page setup they want)
- What functionality are you looking for on your website? (like image galleries, forms, video, memberships, Instagram feeds - this is to figure out what they want, and IF this is a job you feel like doing)
- Do you plan to manage the website yourself, or do you want someone else to do it for you? So you can decide what theme builder to use, Bricks or Oxygen. And if the client would be up for paying you to do monthly maintenance.
- What are your branding colors and logo like?
- Do you have content ready such as text, images, videos, and other necessities?
- What regular tasks do you find boring and maybe struggling with that I could do for you? (another potential recurring income task for you each month)

Very often, new clients who want a website do not have their ideas or even content together at all. So make sure you calculate this into the price you're giving the client. If your job also becomes having a planning stage with the client, it will need more of your time. The reason is that their minds are often focused elsewhere instead of the technical building of their website. They also don't understand the amount of work involved in completing a website project. Not until you start asking the questions.

Later when a price quote has roughly been agreed upon, ensure you get all the content and resources delivered to complete the job. Part of the project is also the initial conversion, the follow-up communication, the planning, creating the invoice, and other in-between meetings you will have. So estimate a certain amount of time for this also when you calculate the time estimate for the complete job.

Last, when it comes to the topic of writing a "contract", that is not something I do. For my part, I don't like the word contract. And my experience is that clients don't like it either. I have almost lost 3 jobs just by mentioning a "contract". Instead, just make it lightweight and simple and write a detailed and clear "Project Description". A recap of what you have agreed to be included in the job. I just send this over as a regular email message, which feels much better for the client. You can "print" out this specific email as a PDF file and save it to your project for reference.

After project details have been discussed and the first invoice of 50-70% has been sent to the client, organizing the project will be the next step.

How to organize your website building process and workflow

Some of my beta-readers for the early version of this book asked how I manage my workflow as a web designer. That's a good question. As I mentioned, an organized workflow will help you earn a better income. Because you're in control and more effective when you stay organized. So, here's how I organize my work in general. I divide my work into three major segments. And then I have checklists within these segments of work.

1. Initial administrative work

- Connecting with and meeting the client to agree on the work to be done and set the price.
- Prepare the first (50-70%) invoice, attach it to the project you created, and send it to the client.

- Set up the workflow in a new project.

Before starting any actual, technical, or design-specific work, wait for the client to pay the 50% invoice up front. This is your guarantee and trust seal that the client is committed and ready to go.

2. The website's technical work itself

- Start the work and complete the outlined tasks for the job.
- Zoom meetings with the client to review in between.
- Note any adjustments and changes to the project. Ensure you are not doing NEW and added work to the project without agreeing to a new price. The added tasks are something you will add to the closing invoice.

3. The finishing stage

- Do a backup of the site before the client takes over.
- Do a finishing Zoom meeting with the client.
- Consider and complete any added work, if any.
- Sum up and finish the last invoice. Add any additional hours of extra work if the client asked for new details outside of the initial agreement.
- Deliver any necessary logins and administrative information to the client.

I like to keep things simple and tidy. This way, I can maintain a simple visual overview in my head. The most detailed checklist for a client web design project will be the task list for building the site itself. So let's look into that next.

WordPress project building workflow

I know this is an interesting chapter for many beginners doing creative projects like web design, copywriting, graphic design, and such. I have been asked specifically about the process for building a WordPress website many times. So

I wanted to include a simple checklist in this book that you can copy and set up in the project management tool that you have chosen. You most likely want to create a template with these tasks so you can just duplicate and use it for your future projects.

Administrative tasks

These are tasks related to the project and cover everything that is not technical.

✓ Meetings with clients
✓ Project evaluation and research
✓ Project setup in PMS
✓ Invoicing and payment follow-up

Hosting and domain setup

These tasks are work you will be doing related to domain registration, migration, or maintenance.

✓ Domain registration and setup
✓ Domain DNS changes
✓ WordPress setup and theme install
✓ Setting up email accounts on the domain
✓ SSL activation checkup

Website project building

These tasks are the main work to be done for building the website. Note that all of these may not apply to your first project.

✓ Set up page-builder correctly
✓ Install plugins as needed
✓ Build out the homepage
✓ Build out all sub-pages (About us, Contact us, Products, Services, Etc.)

- ✓ Set up separate landing-pages (if clients has one or more)
- ✓ Do a backup of the site.
- ✓ Add the client to WordPress with a login
- ✓ Activate cache plugins if any

Now, if you're a complete beginner, does this list scare you? Did building a WordPress website suddenly look complex? Note that this is MY list, and how I work. And I wrote this up using the wording I know and am used to. These things are not complex, it's just that you have not gone through it yet. And as a reminder, everything in this checklist above still does not require any coding or design skills. This is a typical workflow for a client job. Everything will depend on what your client wants and the changes they will make. It will sometimes depend on the hosting company used, what WordPress page builder is used, and other minor details. But if you go for my suggestions on hosting, page-builders, and plugins, you will have a very solid and easy starting point to discover how quickly you can set up websites that are worth money.

This is how I organize my client work to ensure I stay on track, and don't forget to complete any of the details we discussed in the initial meeting. Usually, I also keep a very specific checklist for items that the client has asked for and changes we discuss. Make sure that you create a separate list of NEW tasks the client is requesting you to do. You need this overview to estimate the added work that does not belong to the estimated quote of the initial project. Over time, you will find a good workflow that works for you.

A necessary habit along the way is to write down anything you agree with the client—especially changes and new tasks coming up in further meetings. Again, clients also like to see that you stay on track and make notes on what they talk about during meetings. If you communicate via email, take screenshots of changes, new requests, and things the client said to keep that as documentation for later. The most important thing from now on is that you enjoy BUILDING. I think when you get started, you will enjoy building new sites. And as you see payments coming in, it will motivate you to continue further and raise your skills. (And income)

Encouragement for new web designers.

The right mindset, finding motivation, and having access to simple learning will significantly impact your income.

Let's start rounding things off for this book by summarizing some of the most important topics. If you read through this book, you should have completed all the steps and suggestions I have recommended. If you do, you are already in the game with setting up domains, hosting, and installing WordPress. The next step is playtime, where you actually start building stuff. To try, test, and learn how to build sites in various ways.

Let's do a short round-up of the main seven parts of this book.

- You have registered a new domain name that can become the hub for a new freedom-based business in the future.
- You have installed WordPress with Bricks Builder or a free theme.
- You have picked a tool to make it easy to invoice your clients and get paid.
- I suggested tools to handle and maintain your customer projects in a productive way. Hopefully, you decided on one you liked.
- I suggested a list of typical tools and apps that you should have available to be ready for the work you will be doing.
- I provided you with some important details on how to use WordPress plugins in your projects.
- We went over a rough structure on how to organize a project and what typical tasks a WordPress website build will have.

My goal with this book has been to help you start a journey towards a craft in an industry that is easy to access. With no prior education needed. The learning curve as a beginner web designer is not steep at all. And the success you may desire is within reach if you enjoy the process of building and learning.

Becoming a web designer is, in fact, a valuable and respected skill. It's cool to be able to handle technology in this way and build things for the world to see. With your name on it. Also, there are many different small and bigger branches into other creative fields that can come out of this for you. I think you will discover that over time. Because when working with website design, we operate within a field of crafts that touches on writing, design, coding, client communication, email marketing, AI, and many other cool areas.

You never know. The self-education you're starting now can lead to other venues and income skills that you didn't expect. I mean, I never thought about or expected that I would be offering high-quality WordPress hosting on a premium level. But I do, and it's a very solid and stable income that is recurring and predictable.

This short book has given you a head start as a new web designer. Because, even though it's been more or less theory in this book, you have been getting a whole concept explained in detail around how professional web designers work today. I have given you a good overview of the primary methods and workflows you will use as a web designer using WordPress. It's a method to build custom websites that are highly flexible. And in such a way that your customer "owns their platform." What I mean is that your customer is not paying for or renting a website platform. They use WordPress, which is free and open source. They can modify and change whatever they like on their website. Even the code.

So what is your next step from now on?

Raise your skills, charisma, and charm.

Please continue to nurture your mindset. Put yourself and your dreams above others' expectations. Do what you must to find motivation and inspiration to have a lifestyle with more freedom. Work towards a goal that makes it possible to never have to go to work again. If that is your desire. Continue building websites, and talk about it in your network so that you build up your reputation.

Reputation is free marketing. Then the jobs will come on autopilot

When working with clients, be service-minded so that customers feel connected to you. Being authentic and real is not a common trait with many businesses where the most important focus is just money. Your focus should not be money, but "your best self". You are a product. And if it's good, clients will happily pay for it.

I can testify to having happy clients and how valuable it is. You can check out some client feedback on my website (JohnMac.pro) to see what clients are saying. This is what we want for you as well. Having this brand quality, you won't have to "sell" or advertise yourself. Clients will do it for you.

Clients will pay you for your personality, charisma, and ability to solve problems and ease their challenges. As I mentioned, maybe it's not even as a web designer but something slightly different. Perhaps you will discover you have some other hidden qualities to cultivate which clients will pay you for. Relax about it when you go out today to talk to your targeted customer. Don't stress anything. Most importantly, remember that you are your own boss. You should be in control of the situation and the meeting. If there's a client you don't like the attitude of, ditch them.

Finding more work online?

The well-known platform, Fiverr.com, can be a low-end, noisy, and crowded space. And it can be hard to get decent-paying jobs because so many people sell themselves cheaply. It's also a place you can risk getting shit-clients from hell that you never want to work with in the first place. Yes, those exist. Drop them. Still, you can also find good opportunities. Try it if you feel like it.

Another platform you can try out would be Upwork. It's a more high-end space you could possibly find work. But, in general, I usually do not recommend aiming for these platforms as sources to find more work. Instead, grow your reputation so others can bring you work instead.

Posting your services and skills on Facebook groups that allow job requests can be a method. Just be careful with pushing your offers too much. Many Facebook groups, online forums, and communities don't like promotions. Another way could be to continue working locally in your area and do websites for small businesses. And, of course, in the footer of the websites you build, you will put your name and URL to your own website.

The first thing I can promise is that there is enough work. The second thing I can promise is that you can build websites just as well as I do. A third thing I can promise is that the tools needed to do it are cheap and even free at times. The fourth promise I can make is that you can make a good income from a craft like building websites. So, it's time for you to make this happen and see a new stream of income entering your bank account. Continue your journey and grow your money bag for more freedom and financial flexibility. This brings about happiness in your life.

I can mention again that I have NEVER promoted anything to find more client website projects. Work has always been coming to me. Sometimes in a tempo that has made it hard to keep up. That is also why team members became necessary over time. I have often had clients asking if I know some other web designers that I can recommend. And in fact, when I think of it, I don't. It's a rare craft in my network even though I have done this for so many years. The only place I could suggest other web designers would be to search on Upwork, Fiverr, and similar freelancer websites. Which is a hassle and quickly becomes a research and interview project in itself.

We can conclude that YOU, your skills, qualities, and charm are what sell.

How to build faster and get paid sooner

Nothing is more rewarding than learning by doing. And doing can be done by speed-learning through video.

Since this is a book, it has limitations to what I could show you. Instead of creating a book with 1111 screenshots making it horrible, I focused on the understanding of the current industry and the workflow.

But, the truth is that seeing how fast a WordPress site can be created is best done through video. On-screen instructions with show-and-tell accelerate your build-time 100x and reduce your time from build to getting paid the same. A book is good to give you the foundation. But now that you know more about the craft, the tools, the thinking, and the workflows, it's time to create something.

In this revised and updated version of my book, based on feedback from past readers and subscribers, I can now show you the way onward from here. And here are your next steps to grow fast.

- A new course platform teaching how to build websites you can charge premium prices for.
- Live Cohort training with Q&A and personalized support (with limited spots on each event).

I could just share a bunch of random websites, books, videos, and other cyberspace resources that are not my content. But I would never be able to support you, train you in my methods, or make sure you don't get lost. So, having my own tribe of bright minds and creative people learning and copying my methods to reach the lifestyle they want is more effective.

The first place you will go next is my primary and updated announcement board for learning and resources. JohnMac.pro/learn/

You have just elevated your skills as a web designer and are on the journey towards working from anywhere. Ready to make a living from it?

Continue to the next step in a new creative career and focus on creating new income streams. Watch step-by-step trainings taking you from beginner to a reputable web designer and consultant. Copy what's working and shorten the time from testing to charging your first customers.

You're now ready to learn step-by-step building process and how to put the pieces together. Search YouTube videos. Or, go to my course website and continue accelerating your growth and income.

If you have any feedback about this book, write to **hey@johnmac.pro.**

The response from this book have been amazing. But if you bought this book on Amazon, I would appreciate very much if you gave the book a rating there as well to help share the knowledge.

Create freedom you must...

A Web Design Side Hustle

**Build Websites. Work From Anywhere.
Design Your Life for Freedom.**

To your success 🚀

www.ingramcontent.com/pod-product-compliance
Lightning Source LLC
Chambersburg PA
CBHW052148070326
40689CB00050B/2519